P9-DCU-469

10/06

You and
Your Only Child

You and Your Only Child

THE JOYS, MYTHS, AND CHALLENGES OF RAISING AN ONLY CHILD

Patricia Nachman, Ph.D., with Andrea Thompson

A SKYLIGHT PRESS BOOK

HarperCollins*Publishers*

HarperCollins books may be purchased for educational, business, or sales promotional use. For information please write: Special Markets Department, HarperCollins Publishers, Inc., 10 East 53rd Street, New York, NY 10022.

FIRST EDITION

Designed by Joseph Rutt

Library of Congress Cataloging-in-Publication Data

Nachman, Patricia Ann.
    You and your only child: the joys, myths, and challenges of raising an only child/Patricia Nachman with Andrea Thompson.—1st ed.
        p. cm.
    Includes index.
    ISBN 0-06-017331-9
    1. Only child. 2. Parent and child. 3. Parenting. I. Thompson, Andrea. II. Title.
HQ777.3.N33   1997
649'.1'0243—dc20   96-32531

97 98 99 00 01 ❖/RRD 10 9 8 7 6 5 4 3 2 1

· CONTENTS ·

· ACKNOWLEDGMENTS ·

Our thanks to the many thoughtful, articulate, caring parents who talked to us at length about their experiences as an only child or raising an only child. Names and personal details have in most cases been changed to preserve their privacy; their stories remain just as they told them to us.

Our thanks also to Joan Zuckerberg, Ph.D., for her support and ideas during the early stages of the development of *You and Your Only Child.*

·1·
You and Your Only Child

INTRODUCTION AND OVERVIEW

You have a baby, a dearly wanted child, to general rejoicing all around. Then three years or five years go by, with no more babies. Grandparents ask when they can expect another grandchild. Your five-year-old, perhaps, starts pleading for a little brother or sister.

A neighbor tosses off a casual remark about your youngster: "Well, of course he's used to getting his own way—he's an only child." Friends start having second children.

And you think: Is it okay to have just one? Can we be a "real family" with just one? Is there bound to be something unpleasant or perhaps even damaging about growing up as an only child?

These are very common and very understandable concerns, even in this day and age, in which the only-child family is more and more prevalent—and almost surely, for a variety of reasons that we'll talk about, will become even more prevalent in the future. Understandable because, for one thing, larger families have been the real and psychological norm in our country's history. Statistically, you, the parent now of one child, are likely to have grown up with a brother or sister or two. So, most likely, did your own parents. It can feel odd or "wrong" to you—even if it doesn't to your child—to be raising your own very different, smaller family.

In addition, people may pop out of the woodwork now and then to suggest to you that *they* think it's a bit unnatural to have or be an only child. Again, even in our enlightened time, stereotypes about only children linger on—they're lonely, they're anti-social, they're spoiled. When later in this book you read some of the observations psychologists and lay people alike have made about only children, I think you will be surprised at how vehemently negative they can be.

A woman who is both an only child herself and the mother of an only child, a son now in his twenties, says "onliness" has been a subject close to her heart and often in her mind over the years:

"I don't know about now, but when Ryan was growing up, I sensed there was still a stigma attached to being an only child. I remember on a couple of occasions hearing incredibly insensitive, usually older adults ask Ryan if he had any brothers or sisters, and then, when he answered no, say to him something like: 'I bet you're spoiled, aren't you?' I had heard the same comments when I was a child and remember being hurt and confused by them. The irony is that I wasn't spoiled at all, and neither was Ryan. He's always gotten along well with other kids and never had any of those problems like not knowing how to share or being selfish.

"I still, to this day, feel a slight twinge of guilt or embarrassment when some casual acquaintance asks me if I have any sisters or brothers and I have to answer no. I wonder to myself: Can they tell?"

That mythology, it seems, is still part of our collective child-raising consciousness. That mythology is what we are going to defuse in this book.

A mass of professional research on thousands of children from families of all sizes over many years attests to this fact: Only children do just fine! Over and over again, they belie the stereotypical portraits and in fact usually emerge from the pack with outstanding strengths and sterling qualities. Research studies and my own experience in working with hundreds of families convince me that there is nothing inherent in the "only" status to put a child at any disadvantage. As with all children, how happily and healthily an only develops over the years has much to do with the quality of the attention he receives and little to do with the size of the family in which that development is going on.

If the first purpose of this book is to reassure you that there's nothing unnatural about being or having an only child, the second purpose is to talk about the quality of parental care.

About thirty years ago, a prominent psychiatrist wrote an article for the *New York Times* about the "only child syndrome." The only child, he said, "has his parents' complete attention. . . . His praises are sung, his whims indulged. In short, he rules the roost." If his parents are unable to have a second child, the psychiatrist wrote, he would urge them to consider adopting one, in order that the family have "more emotional balance."

Today, very few professionals who work with families, I believe, would insist that the presence of a sibling or two is a sure-fire guarantee of emotional balance. But there is much that you, the parent of an only child, can do to achieve that balance and to ensure that instead of ruling the roost, your youngster finds his secure and appropriate place within the family and in the larger world into which he is growing.

Partly, that involves monitoring just how fulsomely you do sing his praises or indulge his whims, and tempering those inevitable tendencies when and where a little tempering may be in order. Partly, it calls for keeping in mind what your child, like all children, needs as he moves through the stages that bring him from baby to young adult. And finally, it requires regular self-scrutiny of your own needs and wishes, and what they have to do with being a parent.

Step back, in other words, and take as objective a look as possible at what's going on with you and your child. I hope I can help you do that in this book, which offers both insight into the psychological underpinnings of the parent/only-child family and practical suggestions on how to achieve the best outcome for your youngster.

* * *

First, we'll explore together your own thoughts about becoming a parent, and see if and how some of those *internal forces* affect your feelings about raising an only child. Without question, a parent's attitude about her family's size influences how her child feels about having no siblings.

Many parents these days, for a variety of reasons, consciously elect to have just one child and are content with a decision that was theirs to make. For parents who have a single child *not by choice,* the lack of a larger family may be lingeringly painful.

A little girl approaching her seventh birthday was asked what presents she hoped for. "I just want three things," she said. "A sister, a sister, a sister." Her father reported that his daughter had "always" expressed the desire for a sibling and sometimes came home "depressed" after playing with other children and their brothers or sisters. Talking further, it became apparent that this father himself had very much wanted a larger family and that both he and his wife were unhappy that despite various fertility treatments they had been unable to produce a second child.

Although periodically, throughout childhood, an only child may express the wish for a sibling, I think it is not surprising that that little girl seemed to long intensely for a sister. In perhaps subtle ways, her parents may have projected onto her their own desires and their own feelings that one child was not enough. It's also possible that she was nowhere near as "depressed" about it as her father thought. Many only children, as we will see, go in and out of fantasies about having a brother or sister, and the nonfulfillment of those fantasies is not necessarily painful or traumatic.

In these and other ways we will explore how your own thoughts and feelings may intrude on the way you view your child and how, in turn, she views herself. Be aware of the pressures from your own history or emotions and from the outside world, and you will be able to take charge of them in healthy ways.

*　　　*　　　*

YOU AND YOUR ONLY CHILD • 5 •

I shall refer later to the "glorious sibling." The slightly derisive sound of that term is not meant to suggest that siblings are inevitably anything *but* glorious and wonderful; having a loving brother or sister or two to grow up with is a joy and a pleasure. Siblings often are great friends and allies, and a comforting presence in one another's lives over a lifetime.

Sometimes, however, they are *not* friends or allies or even especially loving. Sometimes they influence one another in hurtful or damaging ways that linger on into adulthood.

What's important for the parent of an only to know is that a child does not *need* a brother or sister to learn about sharing or getting on with his peers or standing up for himself when the going gets rough. The notion that sibling rivalry is the only cauldron in which a youngster masters those lessons is popular but erroneous. With your help, your child will get all the "real life" experience he needs. And also with your help, he will learn how to begin to forge the kind of loving connections and fast friendships that develop in the happiest sibling relationships.

We will in these pages debunk the myths about the only child—that he feels lonely, he is bound to be spoiled, he is selfish, he is an isolate. Much research confirms that these are indeed stereotypes and that onlies by and large are self-confident, well-adjusted, high-achieving, and well-liked individuals.

That the only child so often presents such an appealing profile may be explained, in fact, precisely by the fact that he is siblingless. Yes, he most likely does bask in the full light of his parents' affections and attentions, and he is the major recipient of whatever financial and social resources the family has available. And that can have wonderful payoffs. When parents sagely balance their loving extremes with the limits and controls all children need, their youngster thrives.

He's likely to talk earlier and better than other children, see more of the world, spend more time in adult as well as children's groups, enjoy more opportunities to pursue hobbies and other personal enthusiasms. And much proof exists that the only child is especially likely to develop rich inner resources that are deeply sustaining.

Achieving and maintaining that balance between indulgence and restraint, however, can be challenging for Mom and Dad. It's easy for parents, by their attitudes and actions, to turn only-child myths into self-fulfilling prophecies. They may be tempted, in small or significant ways, to assign their only child a special status—to make excuses for certain behaviors, to compensate for imagined lacks in his life, to be overly indulgent or tolerant.

At a large grown-ups-only dinner party, the five-year-old daughter of the hosts, an only child, insisted on being part of the activity—although a baby-sitter had been hired to keep her company in another part of the house. Rather than say no to what was clearly an inappropriate demand, the child's parents set her up in a sleeping bag on the dining room floor in the midst of their guests. "She hates to feel left out," they said.

Sometimes your child *needs* to be left out; sometimes he needs to be reminded that he is a child, not an adult. And sometimes you need to remind yourself to curb your instinct to go overboard in one way or another with your much-loved son or daughter. We'll explore how the parents of an only can forget those realities and unwittingly and unconsciously foster in their youngster the development of qualities and expectations that define the only-child stereotypes. See if you recognize that you too often tend to engage in one or more of the extremes we'll mention, and consider whether a little adjustment is necessary.

In examining the parent/child triangle later, we'll talk about some special issues that arise in the mother-father-child family.

You are part of an intense threesome! Just as you and your mate will tend to be absorbed in all the details of your youngster's life, so your child will be acutely tuned in to Mom and Dad—because only children usually spend great amounts of time with their parents and because they are not "distracted" by sibling interactions in the household.

When things are going well, when parents are able to support each other in maintaining appropriate adult/child distinctions, that threesome, of course, can be a marvelously enriching, loving, joyful relationship for all. When things are going less well, when parents are quarreling or experiencing tensions in the marriage or from outside pressures, it's tempting and easy for one adult or the other to try to "line up" the child on his or her side. Only children tend to be very savvy about what parents need and to see themselves as central to those dynamics. We'll explore ways you can keep the currents running among the three of you alive and well and functioning to your child's best benefit.

As mother and father, you and your partner may be "coming at" the matter of raising a child from different places. That has partly to do with the way men and women in general have been raised and socialized, partly with what each of you brings to child raising from your individual history and understanding.

Upon becoming parents, I have found, many couples discover abruptly that the man or woman they know so well as a mate is something else entirely as a father or mother. One father of a three-year-old son described his wife as "the most laid-back individual you'd want to meet. Then Benny was born and got to the age where he's toddling around and talking a little, and all of a sudden my wife turns into a drill sergeant—a real stickler for rules and schedules. And I'm thinking: Where is *this* coming from?"

It really is impossible to know—before the baby is in your midst—what kind of parent each of you will be. I have heard expectant couples discuss at length everything they can think of regarding their soon-to-be-born child. They have determined how and when they will or won't take leaves from work, what diapers and formula they will use, who will baby-sit, where they would like their child to attend preschool. But there is no way for two people, however earnest, realistically to anticipate all the subtler aspects of what their individual parenting styles will turn out to be. And often, one or the other experiences a "where did that come from?" surprise.

In the only-child family, where all of each parent's thoughts and attitudes about the "right" way to bring up baby and all of their hopes about what they want for that child are focused so intently on just one youngster, it is especially important for a mother and father to examine their differences and see how they can—most of the time—present a united front.

In two chapters on "keeping the pressure off," I shall offer some practical suggestions on how to help your youngster grow into his own best self, some simple daily or longer-range strategies that you may not have thought of.

Two parents who are investing all their dreams, energies, and resources in one child run the risk of overburdening him and frustrating themselves when expectations aren't met. In fact, when the pressure is off, the only child enjoys a unique potential for becoming a happy, accomplished individual who gets along well in the world. That calls for parents who are able to see where their own ambitions and their child's well-being may be at odds.

You'll keep the pressure off by letting go of your child when and where it's time to let go; by seeing to it that he has his own "space" and opportunities to separate and distance himself; by making sure that you grant yourself the space and time you need to enjoy life as more than your youngster's mother or father; by encouraging your child's friendships with "surrogate siblings" and close ties to adults who may develop into lifelong "para-parents"; by enjoying your probably very smart child's ability to "deal" through discussion and reasoning, while you still trust your own ability to set limits.

Many only children today are the children of divorce, who typically live in one parent's home and spend various amounts of time with the second parent under a variety of custody or visitation agreements. Many are part of re-formed families that include half-siblings or step-siblings.

If your only is the child of divorced parents or if, through the acquisition of step- or half-sibs, he becomes suddenly not quite an only, you will find in later pages some practical ideas on how to ease your child through the inevitable stages of adjustment he will make. Divorce and step-family developments and accommodations can be especially trying for the child without a brother or sister to help ward off unsettling feelings of dislodgement or confusion or sadness. In particular, I hope to urge parents to keep monitoring and talking together about what's best for their child as he grows and as his needs change.

You need, too, to balance what's good for your child with what's good for you. The only child and a divorced parent tend to develop intensely close relationships that can be gratifying and comforting—or can be nonconstructive or even damaging for both adult and child. Says the mother of a thirteen-year-old daughter who is having difficulties finding friends and being part of "a crowd" of her peers: "Samantha and I have been on our own practically from day one. And I think what hurt her and was no good for me is that I made her the total center of my attention. We both tend to be one-on-one people, not great in groups. She was all I wanted, and I was all she wanted."

A child who is "shared" between two homes or has one or more part-time part-siblings can thrive, as long as at least one parent and ideally both are tuned in to his feelings and how they shift and change.

Before we start, I would like to share with you a little of what my own professional experience has been, what that has suggested to me about what every child needs—and what in the broadest terms are the challenges for the parents of an only child.

A great deal of my practice with parents and children and

much of my research work has had to do with early child development, what goes on with children in roughly the first three
years of life. Many of the children I have observed, then, are only
children, even if some eventually do go on to acquire siblings.

In one year-long study, my colleagues and I set out to determine what differences, if any, existed between youngsters who
were looked after by a baby-sitter and those who were with their
mothers. The toddler/baby-sitter pairs and toddler/mother pairs
came to our playrooms and could spend the time in any way they
wished. What quickly became apparent to us, and what is of interest in the context of *You and Your Only Child,* was how differently
the mothers and the baby-sitters behaved with the youngsters.

The baby-sitters were all warm, caring, concerned, and mater-
nal individuals, who responded to the children's exploits with an
overall evenness of tone. If a youngster successfully slid down the
baby slide or rolled a ball across the floor, her sitter might acknowledge this feat with a smile and a "Very good." If the child reached
over to try to topple down a lamp, her sitter might admonish her,
"No, no lamp," and make sure she kept out of harm's way.

The mothers, on the other hand—all also warm, caring individuals—operated at much more heightened levels of emotion.
When Mom watched her toddler go down the slide for the first
time, she'd most likely clap and jump up and down and shout
"Yay!" When the child rolled the ball across the floor, there was
more applause and other indications that she thought it was the
most brilliant thing she'd ever seen. When the child reached for
the lightbulb, Mom became very agitated and deterred her youngster with a loud "Nooooo!" And that mother was genuinely elated
or genuinely despairing at watching her child display a moment of
spunky independence or fearful tentativeness—or in some way act
like what she most hoped her youngster would or would not be.

In the course of that study and others, I have had occasion to
talk to mothers who were pregnant with their second children.
And again and again, they expressed powerful concerns about

what having this new, usually much-wanted baby would do to their first child. Would he feel awful, would he feel abandoned, would he feel less loved? Were they betraying their child by having another? These mothers did not even realize the intensity of their attachments to their youngsters *until* those second babies were coming along.

All those observations confirmed for me what may seem a self-evident truth: Parents *go to extremes* over their child. This is good—the very young child needs to know that someone is intensely engaged with him. And then, for separation, autonomy, and healthy growth to occur, he needs to begin to push off from that intensity and find his place somewhere *outside* the center of the universe. That amounts to repeated reality testing, during which he gets an idea of where he really is and where he fits in.

The arrival of a second child inevitably brings with it a dilution of that intensity. Everything shifts. In practical terms, Mom and Dad spend less time with the child, now the firstborn, because the child-raising activities and attentions encompassed within a finite number of hours must be spread between two children. And some of those activities and attentions will have to be devoted to keeping up the suddenly greatly more complex business of running a now greatly more child-centered household.

In emotional terms, Mom and Dad at once begin perceiving that previously only child in subtly different ways than before. He or she may abruptly seem more grown-up, the big boy or the big girl now. As another little personality emerges, the first child may be seen as "less than" or "more than" the other—less outgoing or more serious than his little sister or brother, for example. There may be more expectations that he will do well in school—because he's the studious one—but fewer expectations that he'll be athletic or socially popular or musically inclined—because that seems to be the area in which his kid sister will shine.

And as soon as that second child arrives, there exists in the home what I will refer to throughout this book as the two-family subgroups—the kids and the grown-ups. Mom and Dad are one unit, child and child are another. In many large or subtle ways, that division has a powerful effect on the ways a parent feels and acts toward her child.

That larger family dynamic, which has advantages and disadvantages, is one *you* do not have. It suggests what I consider the three broad challenges for the parent of an only child:

- *Recognize the intensity of your relationship* with your child, and pay attention to when and how you may need to tone down the bright glare of your focus.

  Parents of only children especially have to be aware of their tendency to overinvolve themselves with their child, to go to extremes; that tendency is there, built into the biological system—and it will not be, in a sense, "interfered with" by the arrival of other children and all the complexities that come with raising a larger family.

- *Recognize that all your expectations,* fantasies, hopes, and dreams are invested in one child. And perceive how easily that can create pressures for your child and for you.

- *Distinguish between the grown-ups' world* and the child's world, and don't feel you're excluding or hurting your youngster by insisting on that distinction.

Because of the makeup of the family, parents of an only child are likely to treat him or her as an equal, as "one of us" or as a peer. The challenge is to enjoy the times you come together as a family or enjoy the mutual dependency and closeness that so often develops between a parent and an only child—and at the same time remember that you're an adult and your child is a child, which means that in some ways you live in different worlds.

· 2 ·
What's Really Bothering You?

OLD NOTIONS, SIMMERING EMOTIONS, AND OTHER ROADBLOCKS TO PEACE

Said a new, somewhat stunned father: "Getting married is nothing compared to having a kid. That's the real sea change in life. You don't have any idea how deeply you can feel until you have a child."

It *is* really impossible to anticipate all the feelings you might experience when you actually become a parent—no matter how thoroughly you thought things out beforehand, how confident you feel in your decision to have an only child, and how happy you are with your youngster. As the parent of an only, you may find yourself, to your surprise, beset by worries, fears, and doubts that seem to come out of nowhere. Some of those feelings may focus on your child and, at least in part, spring from the many unpleasant stereotypes—he's destined to be lonely, spoiled, shy— that have typically been attached to the youngster who grows up without siblings. (When you read in Chapter 5 what we have to say about all that, you will feel greatly reassured!)

But some of those uncomfortable fears or disappointments have to do with you and may grow out of memories of your own childhood, or from deep-seated and only dimly perceived internal conflicts, or from the sudden need to adjust adult goals and expectations to life with a child. And if you have just one child not because you consciously elected to limit your family but because your partner doesn't want another or because you were unable to have more, you may feel sad, short-changed, or angry.

"I'm crazy about my daughter," says the father of a five-year-old. "My wife and I talked it over and decided not to have any more kids, and in one way that's fine with me. But I can't get over the feeling of wanting to try for a boy. To carry on the name, I guess. Also, I keep thinking how great it would be to give my father a grandson. He'd love that. All his grandchildren so far are girls."

The single mother of a now teenage girl, a woman who gave birth to her only child when she was forty-three, worries about "getting old and Rachel feeling responsible for me. My own parents needed a lot of help in their later years. Even though I was the one on call usually, because I lived nearby, I still had my brother and sister to talk to about problems. Rachel won't have that."

All such second thoughts, nagging fears, and mixed feelings are human. You may have some—and you may find yourself facing them again and again. Forces from our unconscious, from daily realities, and from our own history always play a role in fashioning our responses to being a parent. What you *don't* have to do, though, is allow them to get too much in the way—let them paralyze or depress you or derail the happy, healthy relationship you want with your child.

Become aware of the internal forces that can pull you in different directions, and you've taken the major step toward not letting them get the better of you. As a psychologist, I of course believe in psychotherapy. It rests on an optimistic premise: If you work at understanding yourself and becoming more aware of why you think what you think and feel what you feel, you can change things for the better. That's what this chapter is all about.

Before we explore some of the interior monologues you may be having, it will be helpful to talk about how the history and ideas we bring with us into child raising affect *all* parents. Whether you have one child or five, you will have fears and issues as a parent. Consider the scenarios and dilemmas that follow, to see if they have any bearing on how you're raising your only child.

GHOSTS OF THE PAST

Your father was a stern disciplinarian, whose idea of a good child was an obedient child. Now a father yourself, you're determined to show your child the kind of affectionate loving you felt you never received. Or your mother was a genuinely happy homemaker, always there for you, a woman who with seeming effortlessness kept the household going and made everybody feel cozy and secure. And without even consciously thinking much about those long ago days, you harbor a deep-rooted sense of not quite measuring up as a mother, in ways you can't quite put your finger on.

Without question, the parents we had and the home we grew up in constitute the most powerful legacy each of us brings to child raising. Whether you have one child or four, it's as natural and normal as it is inevitable to approach parenthood from the perspective of your personal history. That's all you really have, and aspects of it will always be with you. Maybe you know that above all you are *not* going to sound like your father (but one day you hear his words coming out of your mouth). Perhaps unconsciously you idealize your mother and tend to emulate her.

When obstacles or unhappy memories are connected with the past, you may very well try to repair that history in your dealings with your own child. Parents who have more than one youngster do the same thing. There's nothing wrong with aiming for better, happier, healthier grown-up/child relationships in the new family you are creating. It can be a healing, restorative effort. In my professional practice, I hear variations on that theme all the time. A parent will say: "I never felt anything I did was good enough for my father, never felt his approval. So I'm very conscious of wanting to let my son know how much I love him and how terrific he is, just being himself." Or: "My parents were completely undemonstrative—no hugs, no kissing. I'm just the opposite with my kids."

Trying to repair the past can be troublesome, though, when in an attempt to be not like our own parents we unconsciously go too far in an opposite direction. The father who was raised by a supercritical, always angry parent may wish to avoid anger at all costs. He'll try to be perfect with his own child, never trusting himself to let off steam, always using an excessively rational approach to any differences that arise—"Let's talk about this, Sarah." (Not everything needs to be talked out. Sometimes children simply need to follow rules.)

Anger can be a terribly uncomfortable emotion for a parent who grew up in an angry household himself, but it's a very real emotion nevertheless. And that father might need to learn that it's okay to lose your temper sometimes. In fact, it's good for your youngster to see that Dad can get mad, sound mad, and get over it, as life goes on. Children aren't really comfortable when parents are emotionally constricted or never get upset. It can make them feel unimportant or make it hard for them to show their own anger.

Whatever issues you carry with you from your own experiences as your parents' child, it's good to remember that the facts of your past history can't be changed. And history tends to repeat itself, which isn't always bad. The best of those ghosts of the past *should* linger on in the ways we love and raise our children. But you do have a choice to create your own script with your child. You're not bound by fate or human nature or obligation to follow any old patterns of parenthood or family life. And the more aware you are of what went before, the more successfully you can banish the ghosts you want to—or should—leave behind.

That's a process that applies to all parents. Many of the worries or notions you may be carrying with you from your own history are there to be dealt with—affirmed or overcome—no matter how many children you have. When it comes to ghosts of the past, the difference between being the parent of one child and the parent of two, three, or four is often not of kind but of intensity.

Your conscious determinations to be a less critical parent than your own father was or your unconscious tendencies to run a household just the way your mother did are going to play themselves out around one child.

That means he or she will get the full force of your efforts to repair or sustain your own parent/child history. A busy oral surgeon, himself one of four sons, has just sent *his* son, an only child, off to college. During his own childhood and early adulthood, he says, his parents encouraged each of their boys to pursue and achieve mastery in some area, according to their individual interests and talents. And each became a high achiever and successful professional—one a musician, one a veterinarian, and the third an M.D.

Speaking of his own very bright and active son, this thoughtful father says, with a laugh: "I have to watch out for myself. You couldn't ask for a better kid than Greg. Top grades, early admission to the one college he wanted. He's a good athlete. He's a lifeguard during summers, volunteers with the shore patrol, worked on the school paper. He has nice friends. And I'm always thinking: What, you can't study violin too? It's like I want him to be my brothers and me all rolled into one."

Self-awareness, of course, is half the battle for any parent to ensure that he or she isn't going to take those re-creations or revisions of family history too far into the present.

But for the parent of an only child, certain issues—having to do with ghosts of the past and with current realities—can prove to be especially troublesome. Here are some:

"I WAS AN ONLY CHILD MYSELF, AND I WASN'T A VERY HAPPY KID."

You have your own child or you're seriously getting down to planning if and when, and suddenly you're remembering yourself as that supershy third grader or the empty way your house felt when you came home from class in high school. If your own childhood memories as an only child are less than idyllic, it's perfectly natural to be worried that your youngster will suffer the same fate.

Margarita, a now adult only child, remembers a "suffocating closeness" with her mother. "All through high school," she says, "I needed to call her at some point during the day, touch base and just hear her voice, even though of course I was going to be home by three-thirty. We were so close, always confiding in each other. I was dependent on her for all my reassurance during what was really a pretty unhappy, lonely childhood and adolescence. It took me a long time to break free of her in a healthy way, and I never want my kid to go through that."

Her child probably *won't* go through that, because this young mother came to recognize that her own unhappiness was caused not by being an only child but, at least in part, by the quality of the parenting she received. She was able to stop fixating on the notion that *her* only child was destined to repeat the family history. She eased up on herself and counted on her self-awareness, common sense, and the great joy she had in being a mother to see her through.

It's easy to ascribe one's loneliness to the only-child status. The reality is that you can be just as lonely growing up as one of five or six kids. "Loneliness" really grows from a lack of inner comfort, a lack of richness in one's inner life. And yes, parents influence how successfully a child develops a healthy sense of self—absence of a rich inner life can come from parent-child relationships that have been insufficient or distorted. When a parent is too overwhelming or intrusive, as Margarita's mother apparently was, or too controlling or too negligent, a child can expend a lot of emotional energy trying to sort out what's "me" and what's "not me." That can make it difficult to form a useful or healthy identification with the parent. And *that* contributes infinitely more to feelings of loneliness than does how many siblings the child has.

Awareness really is the most helpful skill at your service. As the only-child mother of an only child, be conscious of any tendency to assume that the feelings *you* experienced back then will inevitably resurface in this new generation you are parenting. You are not your mother. Your child is not you.

"I HAD BROTHERS AND SISTERS—THAT'S WHAT A FAMILY FEELS LIKE."

Maybe your home was a big, happy, boisterous, noisy one. Or perhaps you had one or two brothers or sisters with whom you weren't especially close. In either case, having a sibling or two or more is the "normal" scenario. Being an only child isn't.

A physician in her late thirties and her husband, considering having their first child, had thought long and hard about what becoming parents would involve. They had carefully anticipated their needs and schedules, and their future baby's needs, and worked out ways they could be the kind of attentive parents they wanted to be. They very much wanted a child and were quite certain that one would be it.

Nothing stood in their way except that last item: once the decision to have an only child had been reached, this would-be mother found herself deeply troubled. "That's not a family," she said. "*I* lived in a family." It turned out she had spent her childhood in the Midwest with three sisters and a brother.

Ghosts of her past were shaping a powerful sense of what it meant to have and to be a child, even though the particulars of this woman's life—her career, her goals, where she lived—were very different from her mother's. She remembered mealtimes around a huge kitchen table, with "everything served in bowls in the middle of the table and then you passed them around the circle." She remembered a crowded but cozy bedroom she shared with her sisters, and the small, familiar good-night rituals they enjoyed after lights-out. *That* was a family.

If that physician had not examined her concerns, she almost

certainly would have been in danger of dissatisfaction with having just one child and of not being as free as she might be to enjoy and nurture the family she did create. But she had a clear handle on what was troubling her; she talked it out ahead of time in a conscious effort to clarify her thoughts and neutralize whatever anxiety she was feeling. She recognized, too, that the life she and her husband were building for themselves was very different from the one her mother and father lived, and that was the way she wanted it. And so she was able to amend her notion of "a family."

If you grew up in a houseful of kids and remember those days fondly, savor your memories, enjoy your siblings . . . and don't worry about what your child is "missing." If your relationship with a brother or sister had more problems than pleasures, don't look back with idealized vision and remember a closeness that was never really there.

"MY FAMILY WAS A BATTLEGROUND BETWEEN PARENTS AND KIDS. I KNOW I COULDN'T HANDLE MORE THAN ONE CHILD MYSELF."

"Because my parents so thoroughly screwed us all up," says the father of an only-child teenager, remembering his own youth, "I never thought I would have kids myself or want them. I didn't see how, coming from that background—and being a lifelong neurotic myself—I could be a decent parent. Then I got married, my wife wanted a family, and I said okay, we'll have a kid. *One* kid."

At the same time, this father adds, "I always thought that raising a healthy, happy child was the most creative and joyful thing a person could do." Although it hasn't been a stress-free seventeen years, he relishes the close relationship between himself and his daughter, and what he calls their "mutual admiration society."

Men or women from troubled families who have or plan to have a child often feel a little shaky and lacking in confidence about entering parenthood. Some, like this father, are self-aware enough to be able to say, in effect: "I grew up in such a mixed-up household, it's amazing I even survived. Given my experiences, I know I'm taking a chance here having my own child. I don't know if I have what it takes to be a parent, but maybe I won't go too far off if I stop at one. More than one, I'm sure, would send me right over the edge."

Sometimes, on the other hand, the conviction that one is enough is the result not of thoughtful consideration but of an unconscious sense that "one child is all I can handle."

In either case, there is nothing wrong with reaching such a conclusion. A troubled past doesn't necessarily *prepare* you for no more than one child, but it can make it more difficult to feel comfortable about the idea of raising a family. And in many ways, it *is* easier to parent an only child than a larger brood.

Having just one with these thoughts in mind can be a mature, appropriate decision, demonstrating an admirable amount of integrity and self-affirmation. And those couples or individuals may, in fact, do a very good job.

"I WOULDN'T BE VERY GOOD AT RAISING A DAUGHTER/SON."

If, growing up, you had a particularly hard time with your same-sex parent, you might have a powerful instinct to avoid that kind of relationship entirely.

Carol, a nurse who had become pregnant and intended to have and raise the child on her own, was looking forward to becoming a mother, was confident in her abilities, and felt she had a good support system to back her up. But she expressed a strong preference for a boy, because, she said, "my mother and I had such a terrible relationship, I know I would repeat it if I had a girl." In fact, there may be a tendency for women who have had difficult relationships with their own mothers to experience mothering as more emotionally complex and demanding with daughters than with sons.

If Carol does produce a daughter, however, she need not repeat her own past, unsatisfying relationship. She's conscious of a potential problem, and she's thought carefully about the kinds of attitudes and behaviors she and her mother manifested. Chances are, in the joy of having her daughter she will be able to work through those troubling "it's me and my mother all over again" feelings.

A woman who isn't able to overcome lingering turmoil related to her own past relationship with her parent might continue to struggle with parenting tensions and anxieties. She may find herself unusually tired, impoverished emotionally, drained by the process of mothering, or she may become aware that she's as overly protective or fearful as her own mother was with her. That parent would almost certainly benefit from some kind of professional help—talking to a skilled counselor and adviser can help her develop better ways of meeting both her own and her child's needs.

But remember that history is never destiny. And you have the freedom, choice, and power to forge the kind of healthy mother/daughter or father/son relationship you may never have achieved with your own parent.

"I ADORE MY SON. BUT I WOULD REALLY LIKE TO HAVE A DAUGHTER."

It is not unusual for a parent, with no regrets about and all the love in the world for the youngster he or she does have, to feel a powerful wish to produce a child of the other sex. Perhaps a woman longs for the daughter who, she imagines, will be a joy to dress up or take to the museum, or will become in time the companion with whom she can share her deepest self. Perhaps, as with the man who dreamed of the satisfaction of presenting his own father with a grandson, the longing for a boy or a girl has to do with a sense of familial obligations, "carrying on the name" or gaining status or approval from the older generation.

If you experience such wishes or fantasies, be reassured that they are perfectly human and understandable. And then remind yourself that the only really good reason for having a second child is that you genuinely want *a second child,* be it boy or girl.

"MY CHILD IS GOING TO BE EVERYTHING I WASN'T."

We all want our children to be happy, handsome, smart, honest, productive individuals who find their own truths in life. At the same time, we can sometimes wish, too, that they'll make up for our own past shortcomings. The father who was a skinny or clumsy youngster and never made the school teams urges his son toward the kind of athletic success he didn't achieve. The mother who remembers her own adolescence as a long stretch of outcast misery relishes her daughter's popularity.

This is normal. To some degree, we all reinvent parts of ourselves in our children. An only child, however, is the sole container for all those parental projections, and if your youngster *isn't* the smartest or the handsomest or the most athletic, you can be especially prone to pangs of discomfort or disappointment. Love and enjoy him for what he is, and remember that very few children—with or without siblings—turn out to satisfy all of a parent's hopes and dreams.

Sometimes a parent unconsciously and excessively projects her own needs onto her only child, with damaging results.

An accomplished journalist who has always been somewhat obese considered herself from early childhood the odd girl out— not a hit with boys, not someone who made friends easily. Her only child, Phoebe, now a teenager, has battled eating disorders for several years and continues to express acute unhappiness with her appearance.

Phoebe's mother is a decent, caring parent, but it's reasonable to conclude that part of her unconscious agenda over the years was that her child would be beautiful, perfect, thin, and popular—the girl and young woman her mother wasn't. That agenda probably came to the surface in many ways—in an excessive, overly involved attention to her daughter's eating habits or social activities, for example. And Phoebe paid a harsh price as the recipient of those attentions.

You won't fall into this pattern if you're conscious of all those personal disappointments, hurts, or unrealized aspirations that still can smart all these years later. Don't let them intrude too much in the way you view your child. She is her own unique being.

"WHAT WILL HAPPEN TO MY CHILD IF I DIE?"

The birth of a child can, perhaps not so paradoxically, stir up strange broodings on death and loss. The mother of a six-month-old son says: "I was bathing Eric the other night, propping him up in about three inches of water. I suddenly had this thought that if I fainted or dropped dead of a stroke right then, he'd drown. He was completely dependent on me not to drown!"

Another woman says she never thought twice about taking an airplane before she became a mother; after her daughter was born, she hated to fly and was intensely nervous when she had to, because "if the plane crashed, my kid wouldn't have a mother."

That's a very human fear of abandonment and a very human voice saying: If something happens to me, or to both his parents, he'll be alone. Yes, the grandparents (or the aunt or the cousin) will care for him, but he'll be abandoned in the deepest sense, left with no parent or brother or sister to share his life.

You'll feel better if you remember that these are normal thoughts and that as the parent of an only child you may be especially sensitive to them—particularly at times when you're faced with a critical decision or have reason to think about the possibility of accidents. Don't let them overwhelm you, however.

Take the obvious steps that will reassure you of your child's well-being if you're not around—make out the will, line up the loving and trusted guardians, develop the warm connections with other children and parents that can help make your child feel part of an expanded family of caregivers.

There's another kind of fear of abandonment parents of only children sometimes feel. The mother of a ten-year-old, somewhat sheepishly, tells this story: "Recently, my aunt died a hard death from cancer. At least one of her five kids was with her every day during that last year. One of my cousins told me after his mother passed away that he and his brother and sisters were so close during that time. They alternated chores—one did shopping, one took care of legal matters—and they made a point of all getting together with their mother every week or two. He said they told great family stories, with lots of laughs and good memories, my aunt holding court from the couch.

"I had a terrible, guilty thought," she continues, "that I won't have anything like that. That it will be just my daughter, Sarah, and me when I get old."

That's another absolutely human, normal feeling. Sarah's mother was anxious about the fact that her only child won't have a sibling with whom to share the possible burdens of her mother's aging. Such worries become unhealthy only if a parent seriously considers having more than one child just to ensure more company and support in her old age—or to relieve her child of some future distress.

It can be comforting, of course, to share the concerns of aging parents with a sibling. And it's comforting, too, to imagine ourselves surrounded by a large, generous family should we need help. But there are no guarantees in parenting, as in life, and for every story of grown siblings who are uniformly loving and attentive to their parents, there is one of a family divided by sibling competitiveness, alienation, or resentment.

The quality of parent/child relationships never turns on the numbers of people involved. Nurture your only child as the new generation he is, and stop yourself from brooding too much over imaginary scenarios of abandonment.

"IF SOMETHING HAPPENS TO MY CHILD, I WON'T BE A PARENT ANYMORE."

Many parents acknowledge low-level but deep-seated fears of losing their only child. One mother of an eight-year-old daughter remembers "thinking of that old expression: the heir and the spare. I didn't have the spare! Not that Meg was or is the 'heir' to much! But I was very conscious of having a fear of something happening to Meg—especially intensely when she was a baby. Then I would have no child."

Says another parent: "I did want two kids, but Michael and I got divorced too soon for me to have two. It's not like one wasn't enough of a challenge! But I was always so scared of Katie not being all right, or of something happening to her. Not that if you have two and one dies it's okay, but at least you have something left, especially if you're divorced. If something happened to Katie, what would I have? No husband, no kid."

Meg's mother's sister, with three children, reassures her "that you still worry and you're still nervous—just multiply that by three." And Katie's mother is able to acknowledge and keep in reasonable control those fears about losing her only child. Such normal fears are troublesome and potentially harmful only if they lead a parent to become excessively protective of her youngster, restricting him in his appropriate moves toward growth and separation in an effort to keep him "safe."

"WE WANTED JUST ONE CHILD BECAUSE MY HUSBAND AND I ARE BOTH VERY CAREER-ORIENTED, AND WE FELT WE COULDN'T MANAGE JOBS AND KIDS. IS THAT SELFISH?"

A young professional couple in their late thirties had their first—and, they intend, only—child. Both hardworking, determined career people, they almost surprised themselves by how much they relished becoming parents. They also intend to keep on with their well-planned careers. And one of the reasons they had decided to limit their family's size was that, the wife says, "Neither of us wants to be in the diapers-and-baby-sitters stage for too many years.

"We wanted a baby and we're crazy about her. But we've invested a lot of years and energy in our work. Way before she was born, we had a game plan for where we want to get, and I just think having a bigger family would make those goals out of the question. But now I feel guilty. It seems like this decision is all about *us,* and it's not fair to our little girl that we're never going to give her a brother or sister."

When a couple's decision to limit their family to an only child has grown principally out of their desires to pursue career or other personal goals or satisfactions, they often feel guilty. Are we putting our own preferences over a child's needs? Is it fair to our child?

I have talked to parents who want to continue to pursue their passions for skiing or painting, or want to keep a house in the country, and wonder if those wishes or interests are good enough reasons to have no more than one child. Of course they are. There are no formulas in parenting. You can allow other aspects of your life to be important to you and to bring you pleasure; it doesn't mean you're doing a disservice to your only child.

"OUR CLOSEST FRIENDS HAVE RECENTLY HAD A SECOND CHILD. AND I FEEL ENVIOUS."

Here's a not uncommon scenario: You and your spouse and child have for several years enjoyed a warm, relaxed friendship with a neighbor couple and their youngster, or perhaps with a college chum and her child, or with the congenial pair you met in Lamaze class.

Then that family of three becomes a family of four, and abruptly everything changes. Get-togethers are no longer so spontaneous and unstructured. Your friends want to talk about sibling rivalry, regressive behaviors, and other issues of little relevance to what's going on in your household. The sense that "we're all going through the same thing at the same time together" is gone.

You may feel sadness over the loss or diminution of your once balanced and harmonious ties. You may feel envious, or have the nagging sense that your friends have moved on without you to something more complex, more involving, and more satisfying.

True friendships between families will over the course of time survive sibling arrivals. And there's nothing wrong with taking a breather temporarily and cutting back on your joint socializing if you find your friends' new absorptions and their altered family dynamics a little hard to take.

There's another way in which the arrival of other parents' second children can stir up uncomfortable feelings. "I'm so glad I had two," says an acquaintance, "because you're so much more confident with the second. And I think I'm a better, more relaxed parent now with my oldest." Suddenly you're questioning your own parenting skills and wondering if by not producing more than one child you'll surely do less than the best with the one you do have. This kind of casual input from others can throw you into a spasm of insecurity. The first child is an experiment, people say, the second one is much easier, and so on.

It's true that when a mother has a second child she has a means of comparison. She's a little less anxious, because she's learned that children do eventually sleep through the night and that the toddler who takes his playmate's toy isn't destined for a life of crime.

Can you be a perfect parent to an only child? No, but neither can you be to two or three children. Can you be a nurturing, good enough parent to your youngster? Of course you can, and feeling a little insecure along the way isn't going to change that. In fact, as we'll see later on, being an "anxious," learning-the-ropes parent is not such a bad thing at all.

"MY DAUGHTER IS SAYING SHE REALLY WANTS A BABY BROTHER OR SISTER."

Your five-year-old starts wrapping the pet cat in her old receiving blanket and carrying it around like a newborn baby. Or she talks to a doll as if it were a sister. Or your son is actively, vocally agitating for a brother.

Some only children may start a campaign for a brother or sister. Not all do, by any means. Many parents of only children say their youngsters have never once indicated any desire to share their good lives with another child.

If *your* only child expresses a fervent wish for a sibling, he may want to be just like his best friend, who has a brother. He may be feeling a need to have someone to "defend" him or someone he imagines will want to play with him all the time.

As long as he's well-loved and has plenty of opportunities to get together with other youngsters, his agitation for a sibling will likely pass. His notion of what having a brother or sister would actually be like is in any case based on a fantasy. You might find it comforting to remember that the reality probably would not delight your child anywhere near as much as he thinks it would.

No matter how rationally we approach it, becoming a parent is above all else an emotional business. As you raise your only child, don't be surprised when emotions that can seem to come out of left field unsettle you. Understanding your own history, needs, and conflicts is the first step—really the major step—to unloading useless baggage.

· 3 ·
One Child ... Not by Choice

WHEN FATE OR CIRCUMSTANCE
LIMITS FAMILY SIZE

If you are able to say, "We've decided to have just one child, that's what we want," or, "It might be nice to have a larger family, but we know we can't afford it, so one's great for us," you will probably not find it terribly difficult to come to terms with whatever worries or concerns about only children occupy the back of your mind. If that decision is not yours to make, however, feelings about your only-child family may be more complex.

Many parents yearn to have two or three children, or perhaps even more, but for one reason or another are unable to realize those wishes following the birth of one child. For those adults, feelings of sadness or anger, or a sense of having been unfairly denied what is "rightfully" theirs, can be powerful.

Such emotions are often hard to reach through rational self-analysis or talking it out with a spouse or counselor, after which they can effectively be "defanged" and put to rest. They may bubble on, perhaps at a subconscious level, and rise to the surface as a quick stab of pain or longing at the sight of a household with several youngsters; as lingering resentment toward a spouse who, even unwillingly, caused the family to be limited to just one child; as a subtle but persistent message to your youngster that things are somehow not as they should be.

If yours is an only-child family not by choice—probably for one of the reasons we'll talk about later—you may wrestle with any of those distressing emotions. What is even more important, they can affect how your child feels about himself and the family he's part of.

PARENTAL MOODS AND THE ONLY CHILD

From a very young age, as we'll note throughout this book, your child will be picking up on how you feel. Most children are able to sense quite keenly when a mother or father is gloomy, sad, or angry about something, or even when there's just a low-level and undefined air of distraction or discontent about a parent or parents.

One child may go to lengths to comfort his parent, to cheer her by acting very good or in some other way attempting to cajole her out of an unhappy mood. Another youngster may absorb that mood himself and come to reflect it as his own. Children can tend to believe that how the adults in their lives react has greater validity, is truer somehow, than anything they might feel.

Those tendencies are especially pronounced for an only child. You son or daughter is much more likely than is the youngster with siblings to be drawn into and respond to your moods and feelings. A brother or sister can act as a buffer, a confidant, an ally, or an acceptable avenue by which a youngster can discharge feelings of anger or other unpleasantness. In one way or another, two children or three children who share the general atmosphere of the home and whatever levels of stress or unhappiness may emanate from the grown-ups can help each other through.

The only child has no such outlet. And when a parent's distress stems from her unhappiness over the size of her family— when it's directly related to the reality that she wanted more children—the child she does have can pick up clues that in some way he hasn't quite filled the bill!

Studies have demonstrated this fact: An only child is more likely to be satisfied about his "only" status if his parent or parents are also basically satisfied with just one. In one survey involving only-child families, for example, researchers found that the "intensity of an only child's request for siblings appeared to be strongly related to the mother's own desires for more children."

In that study, one parent, a divorced mother who liked having one child and didn't want any more, said her daughter "used to ask" occasionally if she would have a brother or sister someday, but it "was not a big deal." Another mother, who had been unable to have more than one child because of her husband's disability, said she thought it was "a shame" that her daughter had no brothers or sisters, and felt that her youngster "seems to resent being an only child."

It's easy, then, to project your own disappointments onto your youngster. That father we mentioned earlier who claimed his only child always came home "depressed" after playing with a friend and her siblings was himself deeply unhappy that he and his wife had been unable to have a larger family. When parents are dissatisfied with arrangements as they are, the child, even if her parents act toward her in loving ways, senses that "there's something not quite right here, something is incomplete."

If Mom or Dad repeatedly, and perhaps in the simplest ways, conveys the sense that more would be better, a child is more likely to long for a brother or sister. She may actually feel more lonely. She may absorb her parents' values and hopes, and conclude that there must be something wrong about being an only child.

Whenever the child-raising climate in the family is coming from aspects the parents didn't choose for themselves, when parental anger, disappointment, or depression is pervasive, the child will feel the fallout. Each family will manifest those feelings in its own ways. One parent may be overly protective and coddling, another may try constantly to "make it up" to the youngster in some manner.

Because your child can so easily absorb your own moods and feelings about the family's size, we'll talk about some ways you might help to reassure him of his secure place in your life and heart. But first, it may be helpful to explore how the not-by-choice only-child family might happen. These stories illustrate some of the dilemmas that may be present when one or both parents were eager to have more than one.

"WE'VE TRIED TO HAVE A SECOND CHILD, BUT WE HAVEN'T BEEN ABLE TO CONCEIVE."

For couples who struggle, perhaps for years, to conceive, giving birth to a baby seems like a dream come true, all one would hope or wish for. But secondary infertility—the inability to conceive a second child—can for many parents be almost as sad, frustrating, and painful as primary infertility.

One woman and her husband started trying for a second baby when their son was three years old. Now, four years later, they are reluctantly putting that wish to rest, after expending great amounts of emotional energy, money, and time in seeking answers, never found, and treatments, unsuccessful, for their infertility.

"This has taken a toll on the marriage," she says, "and also, I'm sure, on Oliver, our son. With my husband and me, it seems either one or the other of us was always plunged into gloom. There's been a great deal of largely unaired worrying about whose fault it is that we can't get pregnant again. When it seemed that the problem was my husband's, he abruptly wanted to stop trying altogether. There's been a lot of distance between us at times while all this has been going on."

And their son, says this mother, "has by no means been oblivious to it all. Kids are sharp. He hears bits of conversations, bits of phone calls. He knows his mom and dad have often been upset, and he knows it has to do with having another kid. Even though we try not to let any of this impact on him, I worry that he's getting the idea he's not *enough* for us."

What Oliver's mother and father have found equally disheartening has been the reaction of friends and family to their situation.

"Because you had a baby once," she says, "people don't have a lot of sympathy for you going through all this awful, expensive stuff to try to have another. I think we've been careful not to bore people with all the details. But even my mother isn't very interested. She said to me once, if I really want another child so much, why don't I adopt one?"

"HAVING BABIES IS WHAT I'M SUPPOSED TO DO!"

A woman attending a support group for couples suffering secondary infertility expressed a deep sense of failure in those words.

This young mother seemed to equate her potency—and perhaps her sexuality or her attractiveness—with childbearing. And to her, being frustrated in that wish felt as if she was being denied something that was critical to her sense of self. Having children was a sign of her womanhood, and she wasn't getting as much out of it as she wanted to.

Traditionally, women used the number of children they had as a way of quantifying their success. Even today—as the number of children per family continues to shrink and as the disapproval of being or having an only child diminishes—a woman may feel deeply inferior if, due to factors beyond her control, she has just one.

The woman who has a child and who desperately hopes for another but has been unable to conceive again can experience a terrible sense of disappointment and even profound depression. If she is a devout member of a religious group that prizes and encourages large families, and thus identifies herself within her society in terms of mothering, not producing more than one child can be an especially devastating blow.

Occasionally, too, a woman's longing for another child may be deeply rooted in a need for the symbiosis a mother experiences with her newborn. That woman may have loved the dependency of the baby, the feeling of closeness, during the first months of its life, and may express unhappiness that her two- or three-year-old doesn't "need" her so much anymore. She may be especially vulnerable to feelings of failure or depression if she cannot have another child.

"I WANT ANOTHER CHILD, MY SPOUSE DOESN'T."

A woman who married a man much older than she, himself a divorced father of two young-adult children, gave birth to her son when she was thirty and her husband was nearing sixty. Although she very much wished for another child and although she felt her husband would probably have agreed for her sake, she also knew he was deeply reluctant to undertake the responsibility of more children. Happily married, with a now ten-year-old only child, she still has moments of regret about her lack of another son or daughter.

When one partner in a marriage has raised children already, very commonly husband and wife may differ in their feelings of satisfaction with "just one." And even when the spouse who hoped for more harbors no ill will or blame toward her partner, she may still experience bittersweet emotions about the size of her family.

The feelings between spouses may be more acrimonious, and the only child more likely to feel the fallout, when a marriage is not so solid and when one partner is adamantly opposed to having more children.

"Mary wanted to have more kids. But my feeling then, and still now, is that having a second implies much more commitment," says Bill, the father of a fourteen-year-old daughter. "Two kids—that's the traditional family. So if there's any doubts about the marriage, don't do it."

This father adds that his marriage, while not an overly happy one, has endured largely because both he and his wife are devoted to their daughter. "But in my opinion, Mary has never really gotten over not having more kids and has never forgiven me for that," he says. "And those feelings I think are playing themselves out in little ways that affect Holly. She's overly caught up in everything Holly does. They have arguments about where she should part her hair! The kid is now a teenager, and Mary still wants her to be dressing like a five-year-old. With Holly and her mother, going shopping is always a confrontational thing. I've just set up a small clothing allowance for Holly alone, so that she can spend her own money as she wants."

This father feels his wife's investment in their only child intensified after the girl was five or six. "Before that, Mary and I were still actively battling out this issue of having a second," he says. "When Mary finally gave it up, then this idea that Holly was 'it' seemed to take over."

He and his wife have had very different parenting styles, Bill says. "I tend to be the permissive type. I love that idea that if you give very small children a variety of foods, including all the junk, and let them eat whatever they want, over time they'll come around to picking out a balanced meal for themselves.

"So I was always onto that kind of thinking, allowing for that kind of expression, while Mary was more controlling. I've urged Mary to permit Holly, within limits, to challenge her, to show her independence. But we've never really resolved these differences, and there's been this little attitude on Mary's part that 'I know what's right for our daughter.'"

"I WANTED TWO, BUT THEN WE WERE DIVORCED NOT LONG AFTER OUR CHILD WAS BORN."

The forty-six-year-old mother of a ten-year-old son says she has always regretted the fact that her divorce, when her boy was not quite three, prevented her from having more children. "I have a nice life with Lucas," she says, "and he and his father see each other a lot and his father is very loving toward him. But this was never what I wanted."

For this mother, those feelings that one child can't be a "real family" are strong and lingering. She feels more regret and sadness, she says, about the loss of that dream of having two or three children than about the demise of her marriage. "Especially now that I'm older," she says, "I wish I had more kids because I would just like my family to be bigger. I feel much more isolated than I wanted to feel, or than I thought I would."

There are other situations in which it may be impossible or inadvisable to have more than one child—if a spouse becomes ill or disabled, or dies; if the firstborn suffers from a chronic illness or disability; if sudden and serious financial reverses throw the family permanently off a desired course.

If any such forces outside your control have prescribed your family's size, if you wanted two or three and have an only child not by choice, it will be in your and your child's best interests to try to understand the feelings you are surely having. They may include:

- *sadness,* perhaps a low-level but persistent melancholy or depression over the fact that life did not turn out as you had hoped;

- *resentment and anger,* toward a spouse who is unwilling or unable to have a larger family or perhaps even toward a child whose illness or disability has precluded the possibility of more children;

- *envy,* of friends or relatives whose larger families seem to have been so easily achieved and so taken for granted, and seem to afford the possibility of greater happiness and pleasure;

- *loneliness,* from what feels like a home life that is too small or too isolated;

- *inadequacy,* and a sense that you did not measure up to an expected ideal.

Such feelings can certainly interfere with your joy in being a parent. It is not easy, it is often even quite painful, but when you rigorously confront your emotions, acknowledge that they exist, and put a name to them, they are less likely to overwhelm you or catch you by surprise. And that is the best first step in feeling better about your only-child family.

The woman who stopped at just one in deference to her much older husband's understandable reluctance to produce a larger family is aware, she says, "of twinges of feeling a little sorry for myself, because I love the idea of a houseful of kids. But they're only twinges." She has, wisely, embraced her son's half-siblings, the children of her husband's earlier marriage, as part of her own family and is happy that her only child enjoys their presence in his life.

The second-best step, if you are living with a spouse who may be dealing with his or her own difficult emotions in a different way, is to put effort or better effort into closing the distance between you. Oliver's parents, for example, whose secondary infertility caused such strain, might need to devote some serious attention to clearing the air of feelings about "who's at fault."

Holly's parents, whose differences seem to stem from that mother's resentments toward her husband and overinvestment in the one child she was "allowed" to have, would have done well years earlier to try to reach healthier compromises on child-raising issues. Sometimes it can be all right for the more aware parent to compensate directly to his child for his partner's imbalances or blind spots, as this father seems to do. But it is far more desirable for a couple to work hard at getting themselves in alignment and presenting a basically united front for the good of their child.

Later in this book, we'll talk about ways to open spousal dialogues that ideally will lead to that parental alignment.

And finally, it is good—it is critical—to remind yourself that you have a life beyond the one you share with your child and to make sure that a good measure of your energy and attention goes into it. Lucas's mother, who feels so sadly the isolation and "smallness" of her single-parent/only-child home, seems not to be drawing enough pleasure and reward from friends, job, religion, enthusiasms, or whatever else is in her world. And that may make it especially difficult for her to abandon her dream of children.

HOW TO HELP YOUR ONLY CHILD FEEL THAT ONE IS ENOUGH

Even as you struggle with your own discontents, you want the best for your child. You do not want him to be dragged down, made to feel inadequate or vaguely unhappy, because *your* wishes for a larger family have not been realized. And children are remarkably perceptive. They can read their parents' joys and disappointments very well.

Here are some thoughts on if, when, or how you might acknowledge *to your child* the reality that he will have no siblings, that maybe indeed it would have been quite nice if a brother or sister had been possible, and that you are very happy that he is in your life.

- *Remember that,* as Oliver's mother said, "kids are sharp." Certainly from the age of four or five on, and surely if your son or daughter is likely to have gleaned bits of what's going on from overheard conversations, your youngster may be aware that Mom or Dad or both want another child and are unhappy that there isn't one.

    It's natural to want to "protect" your youngster from this turmoil that really has nothing to do with him. But pretending that nothing's wrong is more likely to have the effect of making him feel his own legitimate perceptions are not true, or are shameful, or must be kept hidden.

- *If your child asks you what's the matter,* or are you going to have a baby, or why was Mommy so sad when she came home from the doctor's, or did you and Daddy ever want to have more children: tell him the truth, clearly, simply, and with care not to blame or denigrate either yourself or your spouse.

    And if your child does not come to you with such questions but obviously is aware of his parents' distress and knows something about what is causing it, he might feel greatly relieved if you bring up the subject.

    Oliver's mother or father, for example, might at some quiet moment say to their son something like: "I know you've probably been hearing a lot about babies, and you probably know that Dad and I would like to have a little brother or sister for you. It seems that we're not going to be able to have another baby, and that's made us sad, and sometimes we feel angry too. But we love you very, very much and we're very, very happy that this is our family."

    So many parents think they must never let a child know that they are sad or upset. But acknowledging to your child your own uncomfortable emotions—without, of course, acting in a highly wrought or alarming way—can be reassuring to him. It can validate his own perceptions and demystify some of the grown-up behavior he sees going on.

- *If your only child repeatedly and with longing* asks if she can have a brother or sister—and remember that she's more likely and more intensely to do so if you yourself wish for a larger family and perhaps in small ways convey that—see if there's a point at which it would be wise to talk quite candidly to her about the realities of your adult life.

A divorced mother, for example, might say something like: "You know, I think it would be nice, too, if you had a brother or sister. But I don't think that's going to happen. First of all, I'm not married. Maybe someday I will be married again, but that's not going to be for a long time. We'll see what happens, but you know that after a certain age you don't have babies anymore.

"You and I are so busy now, with you going to school and me going to work. I love the life we have here, and I'm so happy that you're my daughter, and if we never have another baby in our family I'm still going to be very happy."

If it was not your choice to have only one child, it may be especially likely for you or your spouse or both of you to "overinvest" emotionally in your son or daughter. You may unconsciously pressure your child to satisfy all your hopes and expectations about being a parent, or lavish on him in excessive ways all the attentions you might have wished to bestow on several children.

As you read the chapters that follow, I hope you will find in them some insights and specific suggestions that will help you to enjoy your only child *and* to give him the support and the freedom he needs to grow.

· 4 ·

The Glorious Sibling?
A True Picture

THE POSITIVES AND NEGATIVES OF
BROTHERS AND SISTERS

When parents of an only child worry about what their child is missing without siblings, those concerns usually center on two thoughts: First, isn't a brother or sister any child's best playmate, friend, and lifelong companion? And second, without one, how will our child learn about sharing, fighting fair, and all the other important lessons that come from cohabiting a home with a sibling?

Brothers and sisters, of course, can be great companions for each other, providing friendship and company and a healthy sense that "we," the children, have a life that is different from "theirs," the parents'. But there may be problems in the sibling or family relationships that balance or even outweigh the pleasures, and sibling companionship, in the short term and in the long run, may not always be the absolute good that we think it is.

It's true, too, that when they are young and growing, siblings can help each other along in the critical developmental task that confronts every youngster—learning how to get along comfortably and happily in a world that includes others like himself. That's what all those childhood lessons in sharing, compromising, and conflict resolution are about.

But the fact is, siblings are not the critical factor in that process. Siblings do not provide a child with what he needs in order for him to grow.

WHAT YOUNG CHILDREN NEED

The very young child naturally thinks of herself as the center of the universe. If she could draw a picture, she would sketch herself squarely in the middle, with Mommy and Daddy off to the side—important parts of the picture, but there for the sole purpose of taking care of *her.* And if she could describe her family and how it came to be, she would not know that her parents even existed before she was born.

Every child begins life with such a grandiose notion of herself in the scheme of things. What happens next is that, little by little, she must adjust that perception. She learns during the pre-oedipal and oedipal stages, when she is three or four or five, that her parents have something going on that doesn't involve her at all. She learns that there are other people in the world who are her size and who want the same things she does. She goes through a series of little hurts, really, as she realizes that the world is not quite what she believed it to be.

Siblings offer a natural variable that can help a youngster start to understand and accept her place. But it's really what the parents do that matters—how sensitively they lead and encourage their child or each one of their children toward greater awareness of his own position in the bigger scheme of things. In a real sense, it's a process of gradual deflation!

The best parents will help their youngster descend from that grandiose position, gently, step by step, and in a way that keeps a rhythm with reality. And depending on how well or how inadequately Mom and Dad have mastered this most critical parenting skill, that's a process that can be badly, hurtfully bungled in a family with two or more siblings . . . or can be beautifully successful in a family with an only child.

Still, although you may accept that idea quite comfortably, popular culture—everything from images of Bill Cosby's charming TV family to the number of pages devoted to sibling issues in your child-raising guidebooks—is likely to keep reinforcing in your mind the notion that having brothers and sisters is very important. In addition, you—like every parent—carry with you your own history and perhaps your own rosy or romanticized fantasies about brothers and sisters. And that can make you feel perplexed about whether or not a sibling is critical to your only child's growth and happiness.

YOU AND YOUR SIBLINGS: THE ONLY IMPERFECT, POWERFUL YARDSTICK YOU KNOW

Anyone with a brother or sister or two almost inevitably has strong feelings about those ties—about the whole matter of "sibship," as it's sometimes popularly called. And since the baby boomers are the first generation in American history to have more siblings than children, the great majority of current-day parents of only children themselves grew up with other youngsters in the family.

Whether you adored, hated, competed with, or relied on your brothers and sisters—back when you were all small children together or when you all became adults together—can color your feelings about being the parent of an only.

You may think there's a lot to be said for being an only child because:

"MY SISTER AND I FOUGHT CONSTANTLY."

Says the mother of an only child, a fifteen-year-old daughter: "What never bothered me about having just one was the lack of interaction between two kids. I'm sure the reason is that my sister and I fought so badly when we were little—really viciously. And then when we were older, in college and during the years we were starting jobs and getting married, we had such antagonism toward each other. That continued until really very recently. And it wasn't uncommon among other families we knew.

"So in a sense, I think subconsciously I figured all along that this sibling business isn't what it's cracked up to be, and Meredith may be better off not having to deal with all that stuff."

"MY SISTER WAS THE FAVORITE, I WAS THE OUTSIDER."

Another mother says she tempers her occasional worries about her daughter's only-child status by reflecting on her own sibling ties. "I do feel bad sometimes that Cheena doesn't have a brother or sister. But having a sibling hasn't done much for me. I remember my sister as always seeming to be allied with our parents, while I was the outsider.

"I'm forty-eight now—she's four years younger—and even by this stage of life we're not especially close. She has one son, and we see each other mostly for the sake of Cheena and her cousin."

For other parents and would-be parents, brothers and sisters are very special people in their lives. You may feel your only child may be missing out because:

"NO ONE KNOWS ME LIKE MY SISTER DOES."

The mother of an infant daughter hopes to be able to have a second child, although some factors—her age and her husband's precarious income as a freelance graphic artist—make that unlikely.

"I really would like two kids," says this mother, "because my sister is in some big ways the most important person in my life.

More so than my husband, even! She and I know things that *no one else knows*. We talk in shorthand, because she understands me and I understand her better than anyone. I want my daughter to have that kind of experience with a sibling."

"IT WAS MY BROTHERS AND ME AGAINST THE WORLD."

A man who grew up in a small apartment with two brothers, all close in age, has fond memories of a hurly-burly childhood: "My younger brother and I shared a bed for many years, and I remember it felt so good to snuggle up together. The three of us had our fights and territorial battles, but beyond all that we were the greatest buddies. There was a real sense of the three of us against the rest of the world—including our parents! We still have that feeling."

If your sibling memories and ties are happy ones, you may be especially sensitive to your only child's lack of the same. But even if your personal history leads you to believe that having a brother or sister isn't "all it's cracked up to be," you might *still* be concerned that without one, your only child will miss out on some life experiences and human connections that can't be replaced or duplicated.

Says the common wisdom: Brothers and sisters are companions for life, a defense against the indifferent, harsh world outside. *And* they're a dose of reality and a built-in school of hard knocks, excellent preparation for the teasing, meanness, competitiveness, and other challenges a child will face from schoolyard peers and in the rest of "real life."

Many siblings are all those things. Many are not.

In this chapter, we'll explore some realities about siblings. The fact is, having a brother or sister can be wonderful sometimes, and it can be troublesome sometimes. One child may thrive in the midst of sibling competitions, comparisons, and rivalries; another may suffer and feel diminished by those same family forces.

As the parent of an only child, you may be inclined to dwell on the rosier aspects of what it means to grow up with siblings. I hope that you will come away reassured that having a brother or sister, per se, *guarantees* a child none of the supposed benefits of sibship.

With two or more siblings, the family dynamics inevitably are complex. Possibilities exist for one child to compete with, compare himself to, distinguish himself from, or in some other way "play off" against brother or sister. And as two parents go about the business of raising their youngsters, Mother's and Father's own personalities, hopes, and expectations mesh with each child in different ways. As we will see, these dynamics, in positive or negative ways, can have a great deal to do with how a child develops.

FAMILY ROLES: THE UPS AND DOWNS OF FAMILY LABELS AND SIBLING IDENTIFICATION

Once there is more than one child in a household, each one tends to assume or be recognized by a particular role or label. Each occupies her own place in the family scheme of things.

That label or identity may have germinated back in the delivery room, as the newborn baby's parents observed—and thus, to some extent, perhaps tacitly decreed—that this child was more placid or less cuddly, or louder or stronger, than her sibling. Parents will always make comparisons of their youngsters. It's impossible to view one's children without at some level marking their similarities and differences, and those perceptions tie into the parents' own needs, personalities, and predispositions.

Parents also can label a child according to where he fits in the family lineup—oldest, youngest, or somewhere in between. Researchers these days place little stock in the old notion that birth order—where a child places among the siblings—tells a lot about how someone will turn out in life. Whether a youngster grows up a scholarly sort or an impish popularity-contest winner has mostly to do with a complex and interwoven set of factors, including genes, inborn temperament, siblings' personalities, economics, and, most important, the quality of parenting he receives—and not with the fact that he is the oldest or the youngest child in the family.

Yet the first/middle/last-born stereotypes persist. In one study, over 250 adults were asked to describe the personalities of oldest and youngest children. Almost all replied that oldest children were "responsible" and most likely to be successful in life, while youngest children were less academically inclined but more "likable."

"Oldest kids are just more dependable, I think, because they're more like their parents," says the mother of a son and his two younger sisters. "I really rely on Jake to keep the girls in line."

In many such small ways, parents may react to their children's behaviors with preconceived notions of what oldest, middle, and youngest are "like," or with encouragement of a particular quality of nature or talent.

Taking on a role or label can be wonderfully positive for a child and can serve a useful purpose, helping him feel important and unique, or valued for his talents. The parents of eight-year-old Kurt, who breeds ant farms and has a rock collection, refer to him proudly and fondly as "our naturalist." Being known as "the scientist" or "the show-biz kid" or "the best mother's helper" can give a child a sense of belonging and of his own special enthusiasms and strengths. Even a negative-sounding label—such as "the troublemaker" or "the klutz"—can express love and affection, and impart a sense of identity a child may enjoy and rely on.

This can be part of a process we might call "sibling deidentification," by which a child stakes out his own individual territory as a way of helping himself feel like more than "one of a pack." It's also a way a child may reduce uncomfortable rivalrous feelings: "If I'm not at all like my brother, we're not in competition."

Sometimes, though, an accepted role or label can make a child feel undervalued, less interesting or less admired than a brother or sister.

"I remember the whole sibling thing in my family as troublesome," says Anne, a divorced mother of a college-age daughter. "It wasn't that we fought, but there were little jealousies and little unpleasant things always bubbling under the surface. And I feel very strongly that a lot of the way I turned out and a lot of the difficulties I've had have to do with the fact that I had a sister five years older than I who was the brain—top grades all the time, college scholarships. *And* I had a sister, three years older, who was the flamboyant, flirty, pretty, getting-into-trouble kid who always gave my parents fits.

"So there I was, not as smart and disciplined *or* as cute and rascally as my sisters. And I'm sure because of that, I became the good and earnest and dutiful daughter. The boring one!"

And sometimes roles can "pit" one individual against another, and when a sibling moves onto another's turf or tries on a new role, bitter animosities can develop.

The mother of two girls, twelve and nine, says: "My youngest, Rachel, was a little actress from the start, sassy, funny, loved being in the center of things. Jane has always been quieter and more of a slow bloomer. Then Janie got very involved in writing and last year wrote a fantasy play that was actually produced by a professional troupe at a children's theater in Washington. And Rachel has turned into a miserable, unhappy little monster. The jealousy is palpable."

Sibship was going on fairly amicably in that family until "the quiet one" gained admiration in an area "the little actress" considered hers. And then both youngsters were abruptly plunged into an unhappy new relationship that caused great friction for everyone. When one sibling feels her territory is being invaded, she may work hard to get it back. She may be sarcastic toward her sibling or do risky things to get attention focused back on her.

(When the family is large—three or more siblings—and when the parents are troubled in some way or have difficulty with their parenting roles, there frequently exists a strong tendency for one child to become the scapegoat. Out of their own subconscious feelings of not being very "good" themselves, the parents isolate one child and label her the "bad" one of the lot. And the child acts out and becomes the part of themselves they don't like. I once saw this scenario demonstrated dramatically and disturbingly in our clinic. Two parents and their five young children came for family therapy. All the children were beautifully dressed, except one—who was not clean and wore old and shabby clothes. In conversations with the family, it became clear that this youngster had been singled out in many ways as the black sheep.)

Psychotherapist Jane Greer, who has studied and written extensively about sibling relationships, defines a number of common sib roles: whiz kids (the superbright, gifted, hardworking ones), wonder children (they're beautiful, athletic, or go-getters), underachievers (klutzy, sickly, slow), do-gooders (mother's little helper, diplomat, nurse, or protector), troublemakers (rebels, bullies, and nonconformists), comic relief (easygoing, playful party types), and so on.

All siblings may both rely on and sometimes wrestle with their family labels. Some will be better at this process than others; intense jealousies or resentments may be submerged. Vast numbers of adults still feel "type cast" by their old family roles, and those feelings can be hurtful and constricting.

PARENTAL HOPES AND DREAMS: LETTING UP THE PRESSURE BUT SOMETIMES PLAYING FAVORITES?

One of the great benefits of siblings lies in the fact that the intensity of the relationship between a parent and child will be diffused. With two or three youngsters in the home, one child isn't required to bear the full burden of parents' wishes and expectations. It may be easier for the adults to allow each child the leeway to develop according to his own lights and rhythm.

All parents have a great capacity for fantasy. Every mother and father wants to see a child as a near ideal youngster. In a larger family, each child can supply little parts of that fantasy, and no one feels the pressure to be all things at once. But it can be easier, too, for a parent to feel a better "fit" with one or another of her children and thus for perceptions of favoritism to develop.

A thoughtful and self-aware mother of two sons, aged seven and five and a half, says her oldest boy "sticks to me like glue. And he's always trying to get the two of us off by ourselves, away from Tommy. I'm certain that he thinks I like Tommy better than I like him.

"I adore both my sons," she continues, "but I have to admit that Tommy is more fun to be with. He's a laid-back, cheerful, flexible little person. He's a lot like me. Tim, on the other hand, has always been a tense, sensitive kid. I think I do respect their differences, but I worry that unconsciously I favor Tommy, and Tim knows that."

It's a maxim of sound parenting that children be loved equally, that each youngster be encouraged in and applauded for his individual strengths, that mothers and fathers never play favorites. It's also a truth of human nature that some people—even among our own children—appeal to us more than others. Maybe, as in Tommy's mother's case, one child seems on a parent's own wavelength, a chip off the old block, or is especially responsive. Or perhaps one child is particularly liked and enjoyed for being quite different from his parent—the outgoing and popular daughter of a retiring mother, say, or the athletic son of a father who was always embarrassed in his own efforts at sports.

(In homes in which one sibling is chronically ill or disabled, parental favoritism or seeming favoritism can be an especially potent factor in children's lives. The well child may feel both eclipsed by his sibling, who needs and gets more attention, and forced to compensate for him in their parents' eyes.)

All children in multichild families know when a parent or parents single one out as the pet. Even when parents aren't playing favorites at all, a child may perceive that they are.

It can be very hard on the child who just happens to live with a sibling who's an impossible rival—a brother or sister who may be a caring and terrific child in every way but, through no intentions of his own and no attempts to "star," easily attracts the affections and attention of parents, teachers, and the world at large.

SIBLING LOVE AND LOYALTY . . . MAYBE

A woman in her mid-twenties whose brother is one year older says, "When we were kids, Jay was a constant pain in the neck to me. Then by the time we got to college, all that had died down, and we had real fun together. Now I can't imagine not having him in my life. He's halfway across the country, but we talk a couple of times a week. He's my best friend."

Many brothers and sisters start to enjoy and appreciate each other as individuals and best friends once the early childhood years are past. For others, childhood tensions can linger on. Indeed, in a survey of thousands of adult siblings reported in R. Carlson's book *The Cain & Abel Syndrome: Getting Along with Your Adult Siblings,* 63 percent claimed "unresolved issues" with siblings.

All those early blueprints formed by comparisons, labels, and perceptions of favoritism can remain alive and hurtful years later. For many adults, they can color self-perceptions in ways that box them in.

Some still feel in the shadow of siblings. "Not long before she died," says Anne, the woman who always felt so invisible compared to her more dashing older sisters, "my mother—she was in her eighties—said to me, 'You've always been so competent.' And that's true, I was, and there's nothing wrong with being competent. But I actually felt a stab of disappointment or regret when she said that. Good old Anne, still competent after all these years! Doesn't it sound like a pale virtue, such a tepid thing to be admired for?"

Some experience flare-ups of ancient rivalries when a sibling moves into their territory or takes on a new or wider role. In one family of four daughters and two sons, two of the sisters, very close in age, had always been keenly competitive. Over the years, Valerie had been acknowledged as the studious one and "the go-getter," while Maureen was the social butterfly. In young adulthood, Valerie enjoyed great success as a financial analyst; Maureen married and was soon raising a family of three young children. The two sisters got along fine—until Valerie, in her late thirties, married and had a baby. Maureen abruptly reduced all contact with her sister to the bare minimum family functions. Says Valerie: "I think her nose is out of joint. I wasn't supposed to have a career *and* get married and have a kid."

(Marriage, by the way, is often a divisive event between siblings. In one survey, two-thirds of young-adult and middle-adult siblings said the marriages of their brothers or sisters detracted from the earlier relationship. They felt rejected by the sibling's spouse, or the two just didn't like each other very much.)

Many grown-ups are convinced that whether they were the youngest or the oldest or the middle child in the family has had powerful ramifications in their lives.

"I was the goof-off all through school," says a thirty-five-year-old man, "because to my folks I was the baby and I don't think they really expected much from me. I got away with stuff that my older brothers would have been killed for. It took me a long time and some cold reality to start getting real about work."

A young woman calls herself "your typical middle child, an insecure little goody-goody trying to please everybody. Which is still what I do."

"As the oldest and the boy of the family," says a middle-aged father, "I had to be the best. That was always my understanding."

The power of brothers and sisters to shape us, then, is so strong that some therapists consider coming to terms with it as one of the key ingredients in finally "growing up."

SIBLINGS IN LATER YEARS: SOMETIMES A BLESSING, SOMETIMES NOT

For many, the best of sibship comes later in life, when old competitions and jealousies seem to die down. Frequently, older brothers and sisters find new pleasures in each other's company, and comfort in a shared history.

Swapping stories about what it was like growing up can help brothers and sisters sort out their lives and validate their memories. (A woman in her mid-forties, an only child, says this aspect of not having a brother or sister is what she most misses. "From my own experience, I have very vivid memories from my childhood, to which my eighty-year-old mother responds, 'I don't know where you get these ideas.' Question to my therapist: Which one of us is crazy?" she says, with a laugh. "Brothers and sisters, I think, can help clear up this kind of confusion.")

In one study of siblings over age sixty, 83 percent said they were close or extremely close to their siblings. In particular, it seems, sisters develop the closest relationships with each other. The next closest is between sisters and brothers, and the most distant, between brothers. Both men and women most frequently name sisters as the ones they are most attached to—sisters, it seems, work hardest at keeping the family together.

A difficult life passage that affects many people in middle or later adulthood is the illness and death of parents. Then, having a brother or sister can be emotionally sustaining or practically useful or both, and many siblings say they drew closer during those times.

"I can't imagine going through those last months when my mother was ill all on my own," says one woman. "My brother and I alternated days going to Mom's apartment, and then he and I would talk on the phone each night, compare notes, and cheer each other up."

"Losing my parents two years ago was surprisingly shocking and traumatic for me," says a man in his late fifties, "even though they were old and I wasn't a kid. It brings home your own mortality. Like the front line of soldiers has fallen, and now you're next up. I feel a renewed fondness for my two sisters. I'm glad they're around, and I've resolved to keep in better touch."

On the other hand, many men and women do not experience that kind of coming together when parents are failing. If their sibling relationships have been especially troubled or strained for years, they may still not be emotionally ready to overcome those barriers or may not know how to do so. In addition, the presence of more than one child in the family does not ensure that duties or responsibilities will be equally shared. Many studies have documented this telling fact about what has popularly been called the "sandwich generation," adults who are raising their own families and caring for aging parents: The great majority of caregivers for older parents are daughters or daughters-in-law. Sons, it seems, do not play nearly as active a role in nursing parents through illnesses and old age as do their sisters or wives.

Even in families with several brothers and sisters, it's frequently the case that one sibling takes on the lion's share of whatever caregiving duties are necessary, functioning essentially as an only child in coming to the support of failing parents. Such arrangements can be accepted by all or can lead to animosity.

A woman who for three years spent two or three hours after work each day at her parents' home, helping them with housekeeping and other chores, still feels resentful toward her sister several years after their parents' deaths. "I don't blan brother, Pat, for not being around much, because he lives dov Maryland," she says. "But Susan was right here, in the same to in Connecticut where I live and where our folks lived. Yet while I was out at their house five or six times a week, she showed up maybe once every week or two. I certainly don't regret anything I did for my parents, but it took a toll on my own family. And Susan could have helped."

SIBLING RIVALRY: SKILLS IT ENHANCES— WHICH YOUR CHILD CAN GET ELSEWHERE

From early childhood through adulthood, growing up as one of several children in a family is a complex business. Along with companionship, there may be fierce animosities. Along with love and loyalty, there may be jealousy and feelings of rejection. But as you are raising your only child, you may wonder what your youngster is losing by not being part of that heady mix of experiences and feelings.

Perhaps you and your brother were constantly at each other's throats right up through adolescence, and then you went your separate ways . . . but, you wonder, maybe that's how I learned how to take care of myself and fight my own battles. Perhaps you always suffered in the reflected glory of your very popular older sister . . . but, you think, maybe that's what challenged me to do so well in school and business.

Is sibling rivalry and competition, in other words, the only arena in which a young child first learns life's big lessons?

The title of a recent newspaper article read: "Sibling Rivalry . . . It's as Inevitable as Death and Taxes," suggesting that rivalry between brothers and sisters is perhaps onerous but unavoidable. A quick review of some current popular magazines reveals similar thoughts:

"The Roots of Rivalry: What Sibling Friction and Fighting Are Really About!"

"Peace at Last: Sanity-Saving Tips for Ending the Sibling Wars!"

"Resolving Sibling Rivalry: Surefire Strategies for Classic Conflicts."

It would sound as if brothers and sisters fighting and jostling for place is one of the stickiest and most unpleasant aspects of raising children.

But at the same time, the fact that so much attention and so many words are devoted to the issue implicitly suggests that sibling rivalry is a core experience for a child, a rite of passage or a developmental task perhaps as important as learning to talk or to "separate" from Mom. Indeed, while parents may hate listening to their youngsters' squabbles, most would probably say they think something healthy and necessary is going on. In her book *The Magic Years,* the child psychoanalyst Selma Fraiberg wrote: "The right to have sibling rivalry is so firmly entrenched in the modern family that parents show a tendency in their own behavior to protect those rights. . . . 'After all, brothers and sisters will fight, you know.'"

It's true that a child can learn from all those aggressive and rivalrous sibling interactions. If all goes well, he will figure out how to stand his own ground, fight back when the occasion warrants it, back down at other times. Ideally, he'll learn how to do that without putting himself down or making the other child feel bad. He will get some practice in the fine art of compromise. He will learn that it's no fun to stay mad and that it helps to be a good sport.

It doesn't always happen that way. Sibling temperament and personality are potent variables. And if siblings are of the same sex or close in age, the rivalry is particularly intense and the possibility is great that youngsters can get those "life lessons" too early.

Yes, sibling rivalry is normal, and yes, it can be one way a child starts learning how to get along in the world. But it's important to remember two truths:

First, how successfully sibling rivalry "works" within the

home has to do with many interrelated factors, especially how parents deal with it.

And second, your child can learn those same lessons without having a sister or brother.

SIBLINGS FOR THE ONLY CHILD

As the parent of an only child, you need to help your youngster gradually get used to a world in which he is one of many children.

Here are some suggestions on how to provide your youngster with sibling-like experiences:

FROM A VERY YOUNG AGE, YOUR CHILD SHOULD BE GIVEN MANY OPPORTUNITIES TO SPEND TIME WITH OTHER CHILDREN

One of the best things parents can do to ease their only child into "real life" is to have real-life children around on a regular basis.

"As Justin was growing up," says the divorced mother of an only son, "I was extremely conscious of the need to keep him in an environment with other children. I chose where I lived and where we vacationed largely on the basis of the availability of other children his age.

"I think I was especially aware of this because as an only child myself, I was often quite lonely. We lived in an area where the houses were far apart and kids had to be driven to each other's houses. Justin grew up in a neighborhood where kids could always find other kids by just going outside."

During the younger years, before a child starts picking up friendships on her own, parents do well to arrange play dates, visit cousins, or, as one mother said, "put in long hours at the playground." And one fairly recent cultural development—the preschool—is a great boon to the process of the only child's "deflation."

ENTER YOUR CHILD IN A TODDLER
OR PRESCHOOL PROGRAM

A generation or so ago, a youngster was usually in the home until age five and the beginning of kindergarten, which might have been the first time he was exposed to children other than his siblings. Today, more and more children are in nursery schools or play groups from an early age, and these can provide wonderful learning experiences for the only child.

The mother of a daughter now in middle school returned to her job when Annie was five months old. "I didn't really plan it, but in retrospect, I think things worked out perfectly for Annie," says this mother. "She and May, her baby-sitter, made park friends, so even when she was still a baby she had contact with other babies."

When the little girl was two and a half, her parents started her in a preschool program in their church, a couple blocks from their home. "I remember being worried that she was too young to handle this," says Annie's mother, "but she enjoyed it. And it was just enough and not too much—two hours a day, two mornings a week; the following year she went every morning.

"She picked up a lot, fast. I saw it myself during visiting days, and sometimes Annie would tell me herself what went on. Some of the other kids were tougher than she was, and she got pushed around a little. One big issue for about a week, I remember, was that she desperately wanted to play at the water table, but she said she didn't get a long enough turn. One day I was there, she was the star of the dress-up corner, dispensing outfits to everybody. She had a best friend and a best enemy before she was three! A lot happened for her."

Not every toddler *will* be ready for such a program; two hours, two days a week may be too much for the child who is clearly very distressed at being away from her mother or caregiver for very long. That child may be comfortable in a small, informal play group once or twice a week in her own home, with one or two other youngsters coming for a brief visit and Mom or the baby-sitter nearby to supervise.

But these very young children will learn rivalry lessons—there are other children in the world, other children want and get attention from the grown-ups, everybody has to wait a turn, play goes better if you can manage to share your toys—in a sphere that replicates the home. Reality testing—where she fits in the scheme of things—starts to fall into place.

Preschools and play groups can be wonderful for very young children, especially, of course, when the teachers are caring, nurturing people who will notice and be comforting if one youngster is a little downhearted or jealous because someone else got to be the milk monitor or is hogging space at the water table. These experiences can be more tolerable for the child than interactions with brothers and sisters would be. It's sibling rivalry without some of the intensity, because it happens in a way that is not going to mobilize so much aggression—this isn't all about getting more of Mommy. The youngster can go home, have Mom and Dad to herself, and close the door for a while on all that jostling for supremacy.

GIVE YOUR YOUNG CHILD THE TIME AND ENCOURAGEMENT—WITHIN LIMITS— TO SOLVE HER OWN SIBLINGLIKE PROBLEMS WITH PLAYMATES

Monitor the proceedings when your child and a friend are playing, and step in to stop nasty behavior and reinforce some rules if squabbling seems to be getting out of hand. All children need a little parental watchdogging. (Very commonly, parents of several children will tend to leave the siblings to their own devices, and a child grows up suffering under too much unsupervised roughhousing, meanness, or teasing.)

But as the parent of an only child, you might feel especially uncomfortable about children's aggressive outbursts—you are accustomed to a calmer household—and be inclined to try to end them as quickly as possible. It's a good idea to stay out of the fray and not try to bring a quick end to normal differences by commands to stop or by offering a solution to the children's situation. That can prevent your child from learning how to resolve conflicts himself and also cause him to feel that it's bad or wrong to feel angry.

SUPPORT YOUR CHILD'S CLOSE FRIENDSHIPS AS SHE GROWS

As your son or daughter grows up, do as much as you can to keep on welcoming other children, of all ages, as a part of your child's life. With your attention and encouragement, she'll learn from an early age how to foster warm and nurturing connections with peers.

The mother of a sixteen-year-old says her daughter "has had a surrogate sister since day one of kindergarten. And over the past eleven years, these two girls have been through it all. They comfort each other. They have at other times hurt each other badly and weren't speaking. They have competed for friends. When one of them got a boyfriend and the other didn't, things were strained for a while.

"They tell each other all their secrets and problems. I think there's been a special closeness between them because each is an only child, and because they can get away from each other and then come back together. And I think they will maintain this relationship even when they're all grown-up."

The wish for closeness is powerful in human nature, and it's perfectly natural to assume a sibling will supply company, intimacy, and connection. Of course, there are wonderful sibling relationships, and a close and loving connection with a brother or sister is surely one of life's great gifts.

But siblings very often are not at all close, as many individuals who shared their family stories for this book have illustrated, and sibling relationships can hurt. They can becloud or derail the processes by which a child develops a healthy sense of self. Especially when children are born close together or when parenting skills are faulty, rivalries and competition for the mother and father can be intense and can lead to frictions throughout childhood that may never be fully or successfully resolved later on.

When parents think: Our child needs a brother or sister, what they are *not* saying is: We want another child. And the only reason to have more than one is that you genuinely want to conceive, create, and nurture a new life. Just remember that having a brother or sister is not the only way for your youngster to achieve intimacy, support, and nurturing ties with loving people. Indeed, it is far from being a guaranteed way.

· 5 ·

Will He Be Spoiled for Life?

Debunking the Myths, Stereotypes, and Bad Press About the Only Child

Maybe you have your only child already. Or maybe you've just started thinking seriously for the first time about becoming a parent, and while one child sounds appealing, you can't picture yourself with two or three. Almost inevitably, though, the thoughts arise: An only child . . . Won't he be lonely? Won't he be spoiled? How will he learn to get along with other children if he never has a brother or sister? And so on.

And if *you're* not worrying about all that especially much, there's almost sure to be someone nearby who is suggesting you should be.

The mother of a charming, funny, outgoing five-year-old tells this story: "My mother was over for a visit one day, and we were sitting in the living room chatting and just watching Jack playing one of his elaborate games with his *Star Wars* figures on the floor. Out of the blue, my mother said to me, 'Don't you feel sort of sad for him sometimes? It's such a quiet life he has here, all on his own.'"

Another mother recounts this incident: She, her husband, and their young daughter were spending the day at her in-laws'. Like so many grandparents today, they had raised their own family during the postwar baby boom years, when having two, three, or more children was the norm. This grandma watched Kathryn trying to distract her mom from all the grown-up talk going on, acting a little pesky about wanting to be read to.

Kathryn's mother and grandmother were in the same room, but each interpreted what was happening differently. "Finally," the mother remembers, "my mother-in-law said to me, 'Well, with three kids I didn't have so much time to spend with them. And they learned to take care of themselves pretty quick. They knew they couldn't boss me around!' I realized Kathryn was bored with no other little kids there, and was tired and cranky and probably needed a nap. And my mother-in-law concluded that I am raising a bossy, bratty, overindulged child!"

Another set of parents went for a conference with their youngster's third-grade teacher, who told them their son was doing fine in his work but was having "some difficulty" mixing in with the other children. "She said Matt tended to wait for the other kids to invite him to join them when they were playing during recess," says Matthew's father. "Also, he didn't talk up much during lunch break. This didn't seem like a very big deal to me."

Their young boy, say Matthew's parents, gives every sign of being a content, well-balanced youngster. He enjoys going to school and has several friends he sees and plays with regularly after school and on weekends. By nature a quiet child, he tends to be a listener and an observer.

"There was a pause," Matthew's father continues, "and then the teacher said, 'Matthew is an only child, isn't he?' We said yes, and I guess we had a sort of 'so what?' attitude. The teacher said, 'I just mean he seems awfully timid around other children.'"

There they are—all those notions about the only child, always ready to pop up. He's an only child, so he *must* be lonely . . . spoiled . . . timid. Or a bit of an oddball . . . unpleasantly precocious . . . in one way or another losing out just by virtue of the fact that he has no siblings.

Whether someone else is suggesting you've got something to worry about because your child is an only, or whether you're bothered yourself by vague fears that your only son or daughter is somehow not going to turn out all right, it isn't really very puzzling where all this concern is coming from. The stereotypes that give rise to it are ingrained in our culture. Until recently, the only-child household was such a rarity that your mother or father probably didn't know other parents who didn't have a bunch of kids. And indeed, it's still the case that the majority of adults in this country today grew up in relatively large families.

OUTCAST ONLIES: THE ROOTS OF THE STEREOTYPES

For most of our history, actually, the fact of being or having an only child was considered more than *unusual*—it was thought to be downright unhealthy. In the early 1920s, a professional in the field wrote: "It would be safer for the individual and the race that there should be no only children."

More recently still—just about twenty years ago—a Gallup poll revealed that three-quarters of white Americans thought only children were somehow disadvantaged. And in a variety of surveys over a number of years, an astonishing percentage of parents have said their primary reason for having a second child was to prevent their firstborn from growing up as an only child.

Popular wisdom seems to suggest that while the presence of siblings has good aspects (somebody to play with, somebody to grow up with) and bad aspects (rivalry, no privacy), the *absence* of siblings has only bad connotations. In 1974, a psychologist preparing a study on family size asked undergraduates how they would describe only children. The response: Although they were generally thought to be somewhat more "autonomous" than others, only children are "maladjusted, self-centered and self-willed, attention seeking and dependent on others, temperamental and anxious, and generally unhappy and unlikable."

Of course, these days the only-child family is increasingly common. And it will become more so. By the 1970s and '80s—because of a variety of influences, including more effective birth control, more women entering and remaining in the work force, and changing attitudes about marriage and divorce—the percentage of one-child families had risen to levels comparable to those of the Depression years, which saw a sharp increase in small families because of economic constraints. Every indication points to that trend toward one-child families continuing and intensifying. Writes sociologist Judith Blake, who conducted numerous studies of the effects of family size on the development of children: "the revolution in sibsize is just beginning in this country, with the advent of the so-called baby-bust and the attendant decline in . . . the number of children per woman." Indeed, census reports show that *one in six* women in this country will be the mother of an only child by the end of her childbearing years.

As a parent, you no doubt already have spent time mingling at the park bench or chatting in school with other mothers and fathers who are raising an only child. As your child works her way through preschool and all the years that follow, she will become pals with children who *also* are not going to be talking about baby brothers or big sisters. You will be, I am sure, surprised, pleased, and heartened to discover how many parents *just like you* and how many children *just like your child* are out there! And as you come to know your child's friends—and your child himself—you will discover little justification for those persistent negative stereotypes about the only child.

Happily, we can also offer some good, solid supporting evidence that they are myths, to be comfortably relegated to the realm of other kinds of outmoded thinking about what children need in their lives—that boys need trucks and girls need dolls, say, or that mothers should never work outside the home, or that fathers shouldn't change diapers!

ONLY CHILDREN: A BROAD PROFILE

Many only-children studies have been conducted, especially over the past thirty or so years, as sociologists, psychologists, and other researchers have taken note of the increasing rise in single-child families. The discipline of child psychology has sought to apply modern methods of statistical analysis to tantalizing questions about how and why children turn out the way they do.

Indeed, as psychologists Toni Falbo, of the University of Texas at Austin, and Denise F. Polit, of Humanalysis, Inc., have pointed out, social scientists interested in families and the growth of children have long been intrigued by only-child families because "they provide an opportunity for a 'natural experiment' for investigating the effect of siblings on development."

It's possible, in other words, to try to analyze why a child is the way he is, without having to figure out how much of that has to do with the fact that he has a big sister or a kid brother, and whether the sibling is three or ten years older or five years younger, or is a girl or a boy. It's easier, too, for investigators to look at how parents influence a youngster's social development when the parent-child connection isn't diluted and diffused by the presence of other children in the home.

Polit and Falbo undertook a massive review of several hundred studies that sought to analyze the connections between family configuration and a child's personality traits, focusing on a core of 141 studies that included or identified only children. The studies had been carried out at various times over a span of about sixty years, between 1926 and 1985, and they included, individually, anywhere from 50 to over 45,000 people. The number of only children in each study ranged from 7 to 2,255, and they included preschoolers to adults.

Thus armed with personality profiles that covered many, many people and many, many years, the two researchers looked to see how only children stacked up in comparison with non-onlies in general (children who had at least one sibling); with, specifically, children who came from small (two-child) families, medium (three- or four-child) families, and large (five- or more-child) families; and with firstborns, middle-borns, last-borns, and all later-borns from multichild families.

What are only children—based on all this gathered information—really like? And how right are some of the theories that have been put forth to explain or predict how and why they develop the way they do?

The most common theory, or "mechanism," say Polit and Falbo, has been "sibling deprivation"—spend your childhood without a brother or sister or two, and you're missing out on some crucial ingredient in life, destined to turn out maladjusted in one way or another.

Another common mechanism—only-child "uniqueness"—ties in with popular notions of birth order, or how where you fall in the sibling lineup tells a lot about what you're like: oldest children as independent, high achievers . . . middle ones as struggling for place . . . the youngest as pampered, or whatever. According to the theory of only-child "uniqueness," then, only children are by definition *unlike* children with siblings. Clearly, they share some experiences with firstborns—both firstborns, for a time anyway, and only children get the full force of their parents' undivided attentions—and some experiences with last-borns: like them, onlies never get bumped aside by the birth of a new brother or sister.

So the researchers believed that in an exhaustive examination of the results of dozens of profiles of thousands of children, only children—if these popular mechanisms held true—would stick out like so many round pegs in square holes. Perhaps they'd show up as the self-centered egotists or antisocial oddballs that the sibling deprivation theory seems to suggest. Or, as the uniqueness theory would have it, only children would appear as an isolated group unto themselves, substantially and across the chart different from children who grow up in larger families.

Those original 141 studies analyzed "personality" in terms of sixteen specific qualities, which Polit and Falbo combined into five big categories:

- *achievement motivation;*

- *character* (this included the qualities or characteristics of leadership, maturity, generosity and cooperativeness, flexibility, and citizenship);

- *personal control* (qualities of autonomy, self-control versus impulsivity, and "internal locus of control," or how much an individual feels he's in charge of what happens to him in life);

- *personal adjustment* (qualities of self-esteem, emotional stability, contentment, lack of anxiety/neuroticism);

- *sociability* (including social participation, peer popularity, and extroversion).

So, what did the research show? Were only children the disadvantaged, deprived, "unique" oddballs of the lot?

Quite the contrary. "The results of these meta-analyses," Polit and Falbo write, "suggest that *only children are not substantially different from other children who are raised with siblings* [italics added] with respect to personality characteristics." In self-control, emotional stability, social participation, and the other qualities that researchers were looking at, only children did just fine. In fact, they did better than fine—in the majority of cases, they had a slight edge. Only two out of the sixteen categories showed differences that were considered statistically significant—that is, the results were far enough apart for the researchers to say, Yes, here's where only children stand out. And in both of those areas— achievement motivation and self-esteem—onlies scored *higher* than anybody else.

Only children (especially adolescents, it seems, and especially in comparison to children from large families) aspired to higher levels of education, to greater academic performance, to satisfying and prestigious occupations.

And they felt better about themselves. In the areas besides self-esteem included in the overall measurement of "personal adjustment," onlies and children with siblings were pretty much identical—with one fascinating exception. Grade-school-age children without siblings, it turned out, seemed to be a lot better adjusted than were their peers with brothers or sisters.

Only children were no more or less likely than anybody else to be extraverted. They were generally well-liked. In fact, for college-age children, the results indicated that onlies had a higher level of sociability.

Only children, then, turned out to bear no resemblance to those unpleasant stereotypes. For the most part, they were pretty much like anybody else, and where they differed, they came out on top of the pack.

ONLIES: THE INTELLIGENCE FACTOR

The same researchers reviewed several dozen studies that compared the intellectual abilities of only children with those of children with siblings. The thousands of onlies included ranged in age from kindergarten children to adults, with the majority between ten and fourteen years old, and they had been analyzed by standardized measures of IQ, aptitude, and achievement, including the Stanford-Binet test, the Scholastic Aptitude test, and the National Merit Scholarship qualifying test.

In comparisons of five types of intellectual ability—general, verbal, quantitative, spatial, and nonverbal—only children performed "significantly better" than did children from larger families, especially in the area of verbal abilities. And these results were true for boys and girls from all socioeconomic levels.

In another analysis, researchers found that only children did extremely well in the area of cognitive abilities, which encompassed creativity, mathematics, reading comprehension, abstract reasoning, and IQ. Not only did they do well; they did significantly better than children growing up with one sibling. Onlies scored significantly higher in twenty-five out of the thirty-two measures of cognitive abilities, and came out lower in only three. And in a follow-up on those students eleven years later, in the category of educational and academic achievement, only children scored slightly higher in forty-eight out of fifty-six comparisons, including the numbers who went on to attend college. (The people they married, also, had greater amounts of education than did the spouses of the non-onlies in the survey.)

Concluded researchers: "Far from being disadvantaged, the onlies in this sample appear to be at least equal and probably superior to those from two-child families in terms of cognitive and intellectual functioning."

Other studies have demonstrated that only children's better-than-others intellectual performances, especially in the area of verbal ability, are not necessarily related to how smart or well-educated their parents are. In other words, only children don't do as well as they do just because they've inherited their IQ from intelligent parents and intelligent parents tend to have smaller families.

INTELLIGENCE: THE PARENT/CHILD CONNECTION

If it's not related to genes and not to the presence of siblings, what does account for this measurable intellectual superiority? Most psychologists, educators, and other professionals point to the intensely nourishing only-child/parent relationship. Based on their analyses of all those studies, Polit and Falbo write that only-child cognitive development "can best be understood in terms of the experiences only children have with their parents, not in terms of the experiences only children have never had with siblings."

These are the children who, for the most part, are planned and wanted. Their parents *spend time* with them, because without other children, they have more time to spend. They read to their children (only children, much more than others, report being read to as preschoolers). They *talk* to them a lot. And only children, in turn, tend to model their language on grown-ups rather than on other children (and verbal ability is perhaps the strongest predictor of educational success).

There is another way in which parental interaction with only children can account for those youngsters' higher intellectual functioning. Just by virtue of the fact that they are inexperienced with children and *don't know better,* parents of only children (and of firstborns) tend to expect a lot from them. They expect them to be walking and talking and getting toilet trained and feeding themselves and understanding the world around them at relatively young ages. Parents' high expectations for their children, researchers believe, lead those children to have high standards for themselves and to be motivated to high levels of achievement.

In broad outlines, then, the only-child profile seems to be an appealing one: Here's a bright, confident, socially acceptable individual with a promising future. So why the lingering stereotypes? Fortunately, the richness and the volume of research in the area of only-child development allows us to zero in even more closely on some of the myths. (Those stereotypical negative traits *can* develop in children without siblings, and later we'll talk about some common parenting inclinations in only households and how to avoid them.)

IS THE ONLY . . . LONELY?

Here's perhaps the most common stereotype about the only child. Growing up as the sole youngster in the household, isn't he bound to feel lonely? Isn't it "sort of sad," as that grandmother remarked while watching her daughter's little boy playing a game by himself, that he lives such a "quiet life"?

All parents, of course, want their offspring to be happy. And there's a powerful philosophy at work in our society about what constitutes a "happy" individual, one that brings with it tremendous pressure to "have company"—have a partner, have friends, be with people, *be happy.*

As the parent of an only, perhaps especially if you yourself grew up in a larger family, you may sometimes be inclined to view your child's solitary status as synonymous with loneliness.

One such anxious time came for the parents of now nine-year-old Charlotte, who, when she was five, invented a sibling for herself. "When she was in kindergarten," the little girl's mother remembers, "Charlie told her friends and her teacher that she had a little sister. We only found out about this when we went to a teacher's conference and her teacher made some mention of our younger daughter! It turned out Charlie had given this sister a name and an age and everything.

"Frank and I were beside ourselves. She's so lonely! She's so miserable! How do we handle this?"

Charlotte's parents started feeling better about the whole matter when they talked to their daughter about her imaginary sister. At first, she denied having invented "Emily." Then she said, tearfully, "I thought if I made it up it would come real."

When they asked her what she would like about having a little sister, Charlotte said she could dress "Emily" in *her* old baby dresses and play games with her. They told Charlotte that even if there was going to be another baby, there was half a chance she'd have a brother and not a sister, and it would be a couple of years before they could really play together, to which Charlotte said disgustedly, "Oh, that's no good!" The imaginary sister apparently faded away after that, and Charlotte's parents began to perceive that their daughter's longing for a sibling was not necessarily an indication of the acute loneliness they had imagined.

The mother of eight-year-old Paul says, "He has wanted a brother or sister off and on, and sometimes it seems to me rather poignantly. Once we were waiting for our take-out food in a restaurant, and Paul started playing with a toddler nearby, showing him how to push the buttons on the phone and so on. Walking home, he said sort of wistfully, 'Wouldn't it be fun to have a baby like that? Wasn't he cute?'"

But Paul, his mother says, from day one has been an unusually social, outgoing youngster who has a great time with packs of people around. "He'd do fine in a family of eight," she says, "the kind of family that puts on amateur productions on Friday nights. Lots of noise, lots of dogs running around."

Does he feel *lonely* in his family of three? "I don't think he does," says his mother. "He's an extremely cheerful, happy kid. And John and I have put in long hours at the playground, at Little League, at his school. He's got a lot keeping him busy."

Another parent says she has to remind herself occasionally to "just leave my kid alone! She's fine!" The mother of a nine-year-old, she remembers that in her own preteen days, she used to enjoy lying on her bed staring at the ceiling, thinking, for the most part unnoticed by other family members—except when one of her two sisters came in to borrow a blouse or in some other way break up her reverie.

"Certainly my mother never hassled me or remarked about my lying there—she *did* make herself heard if I didn't get the table set or do something else I was supposed to. Now if I see Marina lying on her bed staring into the distance, it's okay for ten minutes. Fifteen minutes is okay. Longer than that, and I find myself going by her room and kind of prodding her for information. God forbid she should feel lonely or unhappy!"

Probably she's not, and this mother is self-aware enough to recognize that she is most likely projecting her own anxiety onto a benign situation. And Marina, she adds, is a child who "gets passions about things." Currently, she spends hours designing decorative notepapers on her computer Print Shop program, on which she then copies out bits of poetry in fancy lettering. "She asked me how many pages I thought she needed before she could make a book out of them," says Marina's mother, with a laugh. "I said twenty or thirty sounded good to me, but now she's decided it can't be a real book unless it's fifty!"

Many only children "get passions" and involve themselves in singular pursuits that become sources of deep pleasure and satisfaction.

Various studies suggest that only children consistently lean toward more intellectual and artistic areas of endeavor and toward activities that might be presumed to be more solitary, while non-onlies tend to become involved in group-oriented and practical areas.

Sociologist Judith Blake looked at studies of six- to eleven-year-old boys and girls, conducted over several years by the National Center for Health Statistics, which recorded how often youngsters participated in various pursuits—Scouts, sports, or church groups; artistic activities, such as music and painting; listening to the radio; reading newspapers and books; and playing by themselves. Controls were instituted so that the results were not affected by the child's age or sex, the parents' education and income, the intactness of the family, where and in how big a community the children lived, and whether or not the mother worked.

Here's what she found: Children from small families, and especially only children, were more likely to be involved in cultural pursuits, such as studying music. Only children spent much more time than others listening to the radio and reading (the more children in a family, the less time anyone spent in these ways). And they passed significantly more time playing by themselves.

(Many researchers, noting the consistently higher performances of only children and those from two-child families in standard measures of intelligence and academic achievement, have drawn cause-and-effect connections between those performances and the type of activities children enjoy. These kinds of interests, suggested Blake, may "set young children from small families on a path toward academic success. . . . Since studying and other intellectual activities typically require concentrated periods of solitude, the development of a tolerance for being alone at an early age may also be helpful to the academic development of children from small families.")

Many only children, then, tend to enjoy "loner"-type activities. But according to much research, the majority of them don't *feel lonely.* Study after study that have sought to measure how people feel indicate that onlies are no more depressed or forlorn than anybody else. In one survey examining the interpersonal orientations of about 1,800 college students, the only children said no, they didn't feel especially lonely, and researchers concluded "that the lack of siblings during childhood does not necessarily lead to chronic loneliness in young adulthood."

Many adults who grew up as only children confirm that conclusion. We took our own informal survey of only children and asked them: Did you feel lonely because you don't have a brother or sister? Here's what some of them said.

"I don't remember ever feeling lonely," responded seventeen-year-old Janice. "A nice time was when for a couple of years there were two kids about my age who lived on the same floor. We used to keep the doors open in the afternoon and run back and forth a lot and play. But I really liked having my own room and having them go back to their own apartment at night."

A thirty-six-year-old marketing manager was even more emphatic on the subject of whether he felt lonely growing up as an only child. "Never," said Jon. "On the contrary, I remember being very conscious at some point in my childhood that I really liked having my mother and father all to myself."

And many only children look back on a childhood filled with children. "There was never a lack of other kids in my life," said a twenty-year-old college student. "My mother always did lots of stuff at my schools and encouraged my friendships. And we used to visit my aunts and uncles and cousins regularly. So I never felt I was missing out on something because I didn't have a brother or sister."

IS THE ONLY . . . A SOCIAL MISFIT?

Are those book-reading, playing-by-themselves only children doing what they're doing because they never learned how to make friends? Because nobody wants to play with them? Because they don't much like people? Not at all.

Many parents of only children observe that their youngsters seem to enjoy equally the pleasure of their own company and the company of others.

"I started Meg in preschool when she was two, and since that time she's always had friends," says the mother of a composed little seven-year-old with lively blue eyes. "But she's also quite happy by herself. Many times I've suggested we set up a play date, invite another kid over, and she'll say, 'Maybe tomorrow,' or, "I don't feel like one right now.' She just wants to be left alone in her own head, so she can pretend she's Anne of Avonlea, or whatever else she's into at the moment. I don't worry about this a lot, because at other times she clearly has fun with her friends."

The father of a seventeen-year-old only child has always been bemused by the fact that "Caroline's friends call her; she doesn't call them a whole lot. If there's been no action for a few days, she'll call somebody and get something going. But all her life, it seems, it's always that kids pursue her more than she pursues them."

Interestingly, only children tend to rate *themselves* "less sociable" than others. Researchers who study family configurations have speculated that only children may consider themselves less congenial than most people because they feel less *need* for affiliation, or connecting with others. They've spent more time on their own or in the company of grown-ups than other children, and they're likely to have developed sustaining interests in personal pursuits.

And they may have less need for affiliation because of the relatively large amounts of consistent attention and affection they received from their parents while they were growing up. Many only-child families, I have found, are richly warm, devoted units, within which the child never doubts that he is thoroughly loved. When a youngster internalizes those demonstrations of affection at an early age, he may be less likely to seek affirmation of his worth and lovableness from others.

But if only children consider themselves less sociable, their peers think they are just fine. As Polit and Falbo discovered in their analyses of dozens of studies, only children are likely to be just as extroverted or well-liked as children with siblings. And in the National Center for Health Statistics survey, the teachers of those six- to eleven-year-olds were asked how "popular" they'd say each child was, based on how often he or she was chosen when kids picked sides for a game or team activity. According to the answers they gave, only children and children from small families were, if anything, more popular than youngsters from large families. When parents in the same survey were asked questions about how well their children got along with other children or how shy they were, there was no difference in response between parents of onlies and those with larger families.

(It may be, in fact, that only children develop a somewhat better "fix" on how best to get along in groups by virtue of the fact that they *don't* live in a household with other youngsters. One study of elementary school students indicated that the more children in a family, the less understanding a child had of "peer focus roles," or what other children are like. The investigators suggested that because children in large families tend to play and interact primarily with each other, they learn ways of being with peers that don't necessarily have much connection to the world at large.)

It seems that far from being gloomy and isolated kids who are not much fun to be around, only children—despite some proclivities for spending time by themselves—have a generally upbeat, positive outlook on themselves and on life. In a study called Youth in Transition, tenth-grade boys were asked a number of questions designed to measure their feelings of anomie, or lack of purpose or identity, and their feelings of general resentment— how often did they think that others got all the breaks, that they were being cheated in some way, or that the world was an uncaring place? Only children and children from two-child families showed up as having less resentment and fewer feelings of anomie. They, more than their more siblinged peers, also indicated that they placed value on understanding and developing the kinds of social skills that help people get along with each other.

This same group was measured on what was called "richness of past experience." Students were asked to check off from a list of several dozen items things they'd done at least once—acted in a play, sent away for a radio offer, attended a summer camp, played Ping-Pong, seen a circus, visited a farm, ridden a merry-go-round, baby-sat for a neighbor, belonged to a club, written a letter, made a minor house repair, gone dancing, gone swimming, and so on. Onlies and children in small families led the pack.

Certainly the richer, more varied life a child leads, the greater his opportunities for learning how to talk to and socialize with peers who have all kinds of interests and backgrounds. The father of a now thirty-year-old son says: "To me, one of the great things about having just one kid was that we could bring him along with us. Tim got really interested in food, because going out to restaurants has always been a major recreational pursuit in our family. When he was little, I used to take him with me when I was traveling doing research for my books. With just Tim and his mother and me, it was cheap—we could all stay in one hotel room!"

After studying at the Culinary Institute of America with the idea of becoming a chef, and after investigating the possibility of starting a business selling antique manuscripts to collectors, Tim today, his dad says, "is a happily married guy, a father, and a history professor who loves to cook."

IS THE ONLY . . . SPOILED?

A mother of three grown children points to the family photo album as a telling barometer of parental attentions paid or not paid.

Tony, her oldest, has a photo record that starts from one hour after delivery in the hospital and proceeds throughout his babyhood and childhood in minute increments, all carefully recorded—Tony at one month, three days; at one month, nine days; and so on. Anna's second child is also fairly well represented, although the intervals between pictures are longer.

"By the time we got to Judy," says Anna, "we didn't bother!" And there's a cluster of her third child's pictures all snapped on one day when she was a newborn, then a shot of her at kindergarten graduation, and not much else of Judy by herself.

It's a common scenario: The firstborn gets all the pictures, gets all the baby presents from the doting relatives, gets his parents hopping to his every whim and whimper. By the second child (and dramatically so by the third or later child), parents have less time to dance such attendance *and* they're a lot more laid back about this whole business of raising a child.

They *know* from experience that youngsters get colds and fevers and recover, and they eventually become toilet trained, and they learn to walk and talk and feed themselves. Along with a diminution of parental attention, as the family grows, comes a lessening of parental anxiety.

Many psychologists and other professionals have spent many hours and many words analyzing what happens to a child when—suddenly—there's a new baby in the house. The arrival of a brother or sister per se changes forever the relationship a young-ster enjoyed with Mom and Dad. It's a change so radical and so powerful that psychologists give it a powerful name—"dethrone-ment," meaning the loss of status as the sole reigning little prince or princess, now no longer the one and only apple of his or her parents' eyes, with all that implies.

Only children, of course, never suffer dethronement. And various studies have demonstrated, not surprisingly, that their parents spend much more time with them, throughout child-hood, than do other parents with their children—according to one analysis, mothers of onlies interact with their children more than twice as much as do mothers of more than one.

So, is all that uninterrupted attention *good* for a child? Is being the sole, enduring focus of loving, anxious parents destined to "spoil" a child—to encourage him to feel that his every wish should be indulged, his every passing need should be of primary importance to others? Will it spawn a pampered youngster who never learns limits and responsibilities?

It would be easy to conclude that the *less* anxious you are as a parent, the better. Better for you, because it's a more relaxed state of being. Better for your child, because he's less likely to bear the brunt of your "overreactions," less likely to "catch" your anxieties and become fearful, less likely to stay overly clingy and depen-dent. And it would be easy to conclude, also, that the more atten-tion you shower on your child, the more likely she is to become overindulged, coddled—in a word, spoiled.

There's nothing wrong with feeling a little anxiety. It can be challenging. Feeling insecure as a parent is by no means abnor-mal, nor is it bound to create a clingy or demanding child. Nor is paying consistent, loving attention to your youngster destined to spoil him.

Indeed, as we have said, many psychologists believe that it is, at least in part, *because* parents of onlies are so responsive to and focused on their children that those youngsters tend to become such high achievers. It also helps them to develop the internal locus of control that appears in measurements of personal adjustment, because it is empowering for a child to realize that his actions get a response from the people he most loves and depends on.

One study of a group of fifty-six young children sheds interesting light on how mothers of one and more than one child interact with their youngsters, and how the children respond. Investigators wanted to see what differences emerged between only children and firstborn children over the first several years of life. Out of that group of fifty-six, twenty-one children had no siblings four years later, while thirty-five (called the firstborns) had gained a brother or sister by the time they were about three.

At the start, some of the babies tended to be fussy and crabby, some were more amiable and sociable. Mothers who had fussy three-month-olds—babies who cried a lot and didn't smile much—gave their youngsters more physical attention than did the other mothers. More touching, rocking, kissing, and playing, and also more "distance contact"—they talked and made little comforting noises, did more looking and smiling at their babies. By the time the babies were a year old, all were similar in their behaviors. So, presumably, the added attentions from Mom helped the fussy, unsociable babies get unfussy and sociable.

When some of these youngsters went on to gain a sibling over the next couple of years, here's what the researchers observed. The mothers who now had two were doing more touching and holding of their older children, as those "dethroned" firstborns were crying more and demanding more attention. At the same time, the children who remained onlies were crying less—and *their* mothers were doing *less* holding and hugging. But they continued to give their children their undivided attention through *more* distance contact: they were smiling and talking to their youngsters, showing approval of their actions, encouraging them in play, offering directions. And those only children, in laboratory play settings, were less demanding and less upset than were their peers with siblings, better able to tolerate separations from their mothers, and more interested in playing with toys.

To me, those results add weight to my certainty that concerned, loving parents of an only child who respond to their child with large amounts of appropriate attention as he grows are more likely to improve their youngster's chances of developing into a self-confident, sociable individual than they are to turn him into a mollycoddled ingrate.

And as the research consistently demonstrates, only children by and large never apparently distinguish themselves by the kind of unpleasant behavior one might expect from a lifetime of "spoiling."

Continued, focused attention from Mom and Dad, however, can promote in an only a somewhat distorted sense of expectations. The thoughtful mother of a nine-year-old says she feels concerned at times, not so much that her son is spoiled, but that he has an exaggerated sense of "entitlement" within the family.

"Not in the sense of possessions," says Ian's mother, "but in terms of rights and assumptions. Of course, we're living in an age when all kids have greater feelings of entitlement than a generation ago. We had three kids in my family, and partly because of that, I suppose, but maybe largely because of the times, there was a greater division then between the adult world and the child world. You were shooed away from the table after dinner—go play—so the parents could sit over coffee. But you can't shoo away your only child, because it seems punitive to say, 'Go play in your room because Mom and Dad want to talk.'"

Her son tends occasionally to display an "I don't have to do that because you don't have to do that" attitude, says Ian's mother. "Ian's comparisons are mainly with us, his parents. So he doesn't see why he has to go to bed before Mom and Dad go to bed."

Sometimes, she says, she and her husband just pull rank. "I hear myself coming out with remarks that sound like my mother talking. 'How come Daddy gets to pick the TV program? Because he's the *father*, that's why!'"

Asserting your grown-ups' rights from time to time and drawing a line between the child's world and the parents' world will probably be crucial in your household. Later, we'll talk about some other ways parents might inadvertently be feeding their child's sense of entitlement, and how to stop it.

IS THE ONLY . . . A MINI-ADULT?

"What concerns me sometimes," says Karen's mother, "is that our daughter has done so much, gone so many places. We enjoy an active social life ourselves, and Karen is usually invited along when we've had grown-up invitations. We can do things with her that would surely be more complicated when you have two or three children. In larger families, I think, the vacations tend to be kid vacations—maybe not as much fun for the parents, but the kids have the beach or the pool or whatever.

"It's so easy to include Karen with us, and we have great times with her. But I don't want her to get too jaded. I want her to have something to look forward to in life!"

Only children *do* live in a more grown-up world than do youngsters with siblings. Studies have demonstrated that the more children a family has, the more child-oriented that family is. Parents of onlies, on the other hand, tend to expect their child to join and adapt to *their* lives, and they make fewer changes in their personal and social behaviors and expectations than do parents of multiple children.

But the benefits of growing up in that more adult atmosphere, as we've seen, can be great. Talking so much to adults, only children develop superior verbal abilities that lead to superior academic achievements. Being included in grown-up activities leads to a richly varied experience of the world. In one survey of personality characteristics, researchers found that while only children and children with siblings seemed about the same in terms of calmness, leadership, and self-confidence, the only children turned out to be more cultured, more socially sensitive, and more mature.

And self-aware, clear-sighted parents like Karen's tend instinctively to implement or encourage the kinds of "controls" that give balance to their children's lives. Karen's parents make sure she gets lots of "kid world" experiences and play time, and lots of extended-family time with the cousins of all ages.

"My sister has three kids and my brother has two," says Karen's mother, "and we do a lot of visiting. So Karen gets a taste of some family dynamics—a little bickering or jockeying for position, or she wants to play with an older cousin who doesn't want any part of her at the moment. She gets practice at those kinds of kid maneuvers, which I think is good."

As the parent of an only child, you will find your own ways to encourage your youngster to enjoy the benefits of life in your adult world without becoming an unpleasantly precocious "mini-adult" herself. And again, we'll explore later some traps for parents to avoid.

ONLY CHILDREN: THE FINAL WORD

Sociologists examined information gathered by a National Center for Health Statistics study called the National Survey of Family Growth. Most studies of family configuration and "onliness" have traditionally focused on young and school- and college-age children. What, these researchers wanted to know, was the long-range, into-adulthood effect of growing up without siblings?

Their survey concludes: "The decision to have more than one

child . . . in order to avoid having an only child, would seem to be misplaced. No evidence was found of any negative consequences for onlies, compared to non-onlies, in patterns of behavior in adult life."

The picture of the only child that emerges, then, from sustained research over large populations and many years, and from my own professional experience, is attractive: Far from the stereotypes, this can be a bright, comfortable, socially sensitive individual, rich in inner resources.

· 6 ·

"He Thinks He's One of the Grown-ups"

How a Parent Might Turn Myths into Self-Fulfilling Prophecies (and How to Prevent It)

Only children, as we've seen, are decidedly not destined to fit the common stereotypes—the spoiled misfit, the precocious mini-adult, the lonely outsider—that have been applied to them for so long. But often, parents of onlies, in the way they treat their much-loved youngster, can unwittingly set up the possibility that stereotype becomes reality.

Here are some ways a parent might assign his youngster a special-case status that does no one any good.

"SHE'S MY ONLY BABY—WHY SHOULDN'T I INDULGE HER?"

"Right from the time Kimberly was born," says the mother of a fourteen-year-old daughter, "I was tempted to *get* her everything! For her first Christmas, I bought her a handmade cloth doll, with a little embroidered face and a lace collar, a very special, delicate, exquisite doll. It cost forty-five dollars, and I remember distinctly thinking at the time: This is crazy. Number one, I can't afford this. Number two, she's nine months old! But also: This is going to be my only chance."

Kimberly's mother maintained that rationalization throughout her daughter's childhood, and sometimes now she wishes she hadn't. "Giving her things was always a pleasure for me, but I know I went overboard a lot. We're not well-off at all, and I spent more money than I should have. The other day, Kim came to me with one of the mail order catalogs she pores over, and she wanted me to order a particular camisole top for her. We were kidding around about it, and I said, 'Why should I do this?' And she said, 'Because you love me and I'm your darling daughter and your one and only child.'"

What concerns this mother, she says, is "not that she's really spoiled, because she's not obnoxious about things if she doesn't get what she wants. But I think that because of my overindulgence, Kim doesn't have a very realistic sense of money, of what we can and can't do as a family. This worries me, as we're getting toward the college years and she's going to have to learn to be independent."

IF YOU SEE YOURSELF IN THIS PICTURE . . .

As the parent of one child, it may be most tempting for you to overindulge your youngster with *things*. Even if your financial resources are limited, they will stretch much further than would be possible with two or three children in the home. And it's common and understandable for a parent to have that "she's my only one, why not go a little overboard?" feeling.

It's a good idea to resist that temptation as much as possible. Quite obviously, overindulging can have the effect of promoting that stereotype of the only being spoiled, at least in terms of having and getting things. The child easily comes to expect the most.

But showering your child with gifts can have another, even more hurtful effect. The child can come to suspect that there's something wrong with him. He starts to believe either that, "I'm so good that I deserve all this (but secretly, sometimes I don't feel

I'm very good at all and so I don't really deserve all this)" or that "Mom must not think I'm very good, because she has to keep giving me things to make me feel better about myself."

Being indulged, then, sets up feelings and conflicts that tie in directly to his self-esteem. And although deep down this makes him uncomfortable and he really does not want to be caught up in that circular system, he will promote it anyway—because, of course, all kids love getting things.

He may even come to use a parent's indulgence as a test of his self-worth. "I want this," he demands, and then if Mom or Dad grants him his request, his conflict is reinforced: "I must be very good (even better than I think I am)," or, "I must not be so good, because they have to keep boosting me up with presents." Children, of course, don't have those particular thought processes, but the dynamic is there, and it can cause guilt and discomfort.

Remember, too, that a young child tends to view gifts as a reward for something or as the objects that accompany very special occasions.

The mother of a seven-year-old only child recounts this experience: "One day I saw an adorable little doll carriage in a toy shop, and impulsively I bought it for Emma, rushed home with it, and gave it to her right then and there. Emma was just four, and she loved pushing things and taking her stuffed Kermit for a walk with us. I couldn't wait for her to have this carriage and for us to go out with it."

Her little girl's response gave her pause. "Emma looked at it but didn't go rushing right over to try it out. Then she said, 'What is this for?' I could see the little wheels turning in her head. She liked it, but she knew it wasn't her birthday or Christmas or anything, so why was she getting this present?"

Says Emma's mother: "Getting her special things has always been such a joy for me—really, I do it for my own pleasure as much as anything. But I think I would have done better to put that carriage aside for some occasion."

Children don't like feeling that they're getting "too much." Be cautious about all those extras. Ask yourself, "Would I be doing this if I had two or three or four kids?"

Overindulgence with "things" can lead to a certain kind of "spoiling," of course. It can also promote an unrealistic sense of the family's wealth. Most important, it can affect a child's self-esteem in unsettling ways.

"WE PLAY FOR HOURS, JUST LIKE I'M HIS BROTHER/HER SISTER."

With no built-in potential playmate in the form of a sibling in the household, an only child tends to seek out Mom and Dad to spend time with him. Parents of only children do spend proportionately more hours with their youngsters than do other parents, which overall is good for those children and enjoyable for those parents.

Sometimes, though, you may feel you have to compensate for what your child is "missing" by acting like a surrogate sibling yourself. Joseph, the father of a teenage son, remembers in particular one period during his son's childhood.

"I did some dopey things with Sean, I realize now, in an effort, I guess, to give him the 'feel' of what it's like to have a brother around," he says. Himself an enthusiastic participant in various self-improvement and psychotherapeutic programs, Joseph was especially sensitive to his only child's emotional growth and remembers "sometimes getting hung up on the idea that Sean wasn't getting what he needed developmentally because he didn't have that sibling experience going on." He recounts this episode, more than a little ruefully:

"In one of the alternative therapy exercises I went to, two people were supposed to sit in chairs facing each other. The idea was that you can't talk, but you look at each other and see what, if any, kind of contact you make. Maybe you just look and smile, maybe you touch hands, whatever. The fellow I was paired with had already stated that he was an only child.

"At some point I reached over and started a little arm wrestling. This was something my brother and I used to do all the time—we'd play-fight or play-wrestle. We were like bear cubs, always tumbling around with each other. Now this other guy didn't know what to make of it. He got a little defensive, strengthened his grip, then I strengthened mine, and the whole thing got very much less playful. Later, we discussed it. To me, it was horsing around. To him, it seemed uncomfortable or maybe even a little threatening. I got the idea he hadn't had much experience with that kind of physical chumminess, he was standoffish. So *then* I got obsessed with the idea that I should start wrestling with Sean, because he didn't have a brother to do that with."

What this father remembers developing from that concern was a series of "very artificial, very strained attempts on my part to get my eight-year-old son engaged in horseplay with me. Finally, I caught on that he really did not want any part of this kind of stuff."

IF YOU SEE YOURSELF IN THIS PICTURE . . .

Children really don't like it when parents try to be "one of us." Teenagers, of course, are notoriously appalled at a parent's efforts to act young or be overly familiar in an attempt to get close or to build bridges that they, Mom and Dad, feel are lacking. But children of any age feel uncomfortable when parents stop acting like parents and start acting like kids.

Perhaps especially if you yourself grew up happily with siblings, you may be particularly vulnerable to a temptation to "supply what's missing" for your own youngster, and go to great efforts to become a play pal as well as a parent. Enjoy doing things with your child, of course, but don't turn yourself into a sibling substitute for him; the perception that he needs you to be that comes from you, not from him.

The mother of a seven-year-old daughter shares an experience almost identical to Joseph's. "When I was about Lyn's age, my sister and I used to spend hours working on our dollhouse together," she says, "decorating the rooms and making up little stories about the house. Lyn now has a dollhouse that she enjoys very much, and for a while I thought I should play at this with her. I'd join her on the floor, and we'd rearrange things and pretend this little doll was the maid and that little doll was the visiting aunt or whatever."

Like Joseph, this parent came to feel her efforts weren't going over too well. "It felt forced. My voice didn't even sound like me! And Lyn picked up on this, I think, because we'd usually end up with each of us really kind of playing by ourselves at this game," she says. "I decided that this was not my thing, that I was trying to re-create something for her out of my own past, and that I should just give it up. She and I do lots of other things together that we both have fun at."

"I TELL HER EVERYTHING—WE'RE MORE LIKE SISTERS THAN MOTHER AND DAUGHTER."

Another way in which the parent of an only might blur the adult/child boundaries is not by contorting herself into a sibling substitute but by seeing her child as a companion for her. Such intense bonding on an equal plane can be especially tempting for the single parent of a young or midadolescent of the same sex.

Margot's mother has raised her daughter virtually on her own since she was divorced shortly after the child's birth. The two have been inseparable, and even as a youngster, Margot was privy to most of what was going on in her mother's life. Her mother always referred to her as "my girlfriend" and often dressed them alike. Margot turned fourteen—and almost overnight the devotion she had always demonstrated toward her mom turned to black rage. The two are battling through some ferocious times, with Margot defying her mother in hurtful ways and with her mother devastated by overwhelming feelings of abandonment and loneliness.

Treating a child as a "sister" or "brother" or grown-up companion can have the effect of reinforcing the stereotype of the only as a mini-adult. But even more significantly, it can lead to the kind of damaged relationship that has evolved between Margot and her parent. It's easy to understand how that dynamic developed—mother and daughter, two females, building a life together with very little presence from the child's father. And adolescence, of course, is usually a time of rebellion and difficulty in any household. But because she became the container for all her mother's emotional needs, Margot's efforts to distance herself may be especially hard and angry.

Another divorced parent feels her own similar mother/daughter relationship was a critical factor in the years of reckless, dangerous, destructive behavior from which her now almost eighteen-year-old child is just emerging.

"Erin used to say to everybody all the time, 'Mom and me, we're a team.' I always thought that was very sweet, but I know that too many times I crossed the line between parent and child," she says. "I've confided in her about things in my personal life that were wildly inappropriate to confide to a child. I blame myself for a lot of the confusion that Erin endured."

IF YOU SEE YOURSELF IN THIS PICTURE . . .

Just as children don't like it when parents play substitute sibling, they are deeply uncomfortable when encouraged to assume that role with a mother or father. And parents of only children, especially single parents, almost can't help this tendency to turn the child into a peer companion, unless they consciously think about it—and determine not to do it.

A child needs to feel her parent or parents are in control. Knowing there's someone bigger, stronger, and in charge in her life is what helps her feel safe, and feeling safe is what enables her to dare to venture forth into her own future. But although it may be scary and uncomfortable, a loving child will be responsive to a parent's neediness.

For example, studies have demonstrated that if a mother is depressed, even a very young child has a built-in mechanism that causes her to do something to bring the parent out of her unhappiness. That tiny child will coo more, make smiling faces, or in some other way attempt to pull her parent in. The child feels responsible, and acts in a way that constitutes a reversal of roles.

Remain in a loving but adult relationship with your child—you're the parent; she's the child. Especially if you are a single parent, do be aware of inclinations to "cross the line" between adult and child in the way you make your son or daughter part of your own emotional life. Later on, we'll offer some ideas about how divorced parents can both enjoy a child's company and give him the reassurance he needs that he really is the child and the parent really is the parent.

"HE SITS WITH US—HE THINKS HE BELONGS WITH THE GROWN-UPS."

At a large dinner party, one table was set up for the adults and another table was put out in the family room for the children. One young boy, an only child, insisted on eating at the parents' table, which his mother found endearing. "He thinks he belongs with us, not with the other kids," she said, with a smile. "Who can blame him?"

Another only, a particularly verbal six-year-old, liked to tell anyone who would listen what she and her parents were doing or planning, suggesting by her manner and choice of words that she and her folks were a unit of peers. "My mom and dad and I are buying a house in the country," she announced once, "but we're not sure exactly what house we want." Her father said, "Valerie has had some really good input and good ideas on houses."

Parents often treat their only child as a peer, including her in their activities, talking to her on an adult level. Of course, there's nothing wrong with occasionally allowing a youngster to take part in grown-up affairs and family decisions. The danger lies in encouraging that kind of involvement to an inappropriate degree, so that the child becomes part of the couple, and the separation between the grown-up world and the child world is obliterated. That can turn the youngster into the kind of unpleasantly preco-cious "mini-adult" of the only-child stereotype. It can also have damaging long-term effects on how she develops.

A man now in his mid-thirties grew up as the only child of lively, entertaining, adoring parents who, in effect, made him one of them. Even as a very young child, as far back as nursery school and kindergarten, he enjoyed being with his parents more than he did with other children, and was always eager to get home to play with his mother, who was a delightful companion to her little boy. This yearning to be back with his parent was not a reflection of a typical and normal period of separation anxiety—he just liked it better.

Mother and son enjoyed visiting museums and baking bread together. On most evenings, Mom, Dad, and son played board games and card games, and on Friday nights all three stayed up late, watching old movies on TV.

As he grew, his parents made him so much a part of their own lives that when, occasionally, they went out and—appropri-ately—left him home, he felt deeply hurt and excluded. Throughout his childhood he devoted much energy to trying to join his mother and father in all their activities. He made some friends, but never in a real sense threw his lot in with his peers.

As a young adult now, he's still wrestling with some terribly difficult problems. Although he's established in a comfortable career and maintains his own apartment, he spends much of his time at his parents' home. He recognizes that he must distance himself from Mom and Dad, and wants to do so. He makes himself take part in activities with people his own age but can never quite relinquish that longing for the kind of intensely close, loving good times he had with his parents.

All along his road in life, he never made a true investment in developing a world among his peers. And his parents contributed to that dilemma by always treating their son as part of their twosome.

IF YOU SEE YOURSELF IN THIS PICTURE . . .

One of the functions of siblings is that with two or more children, the home becomes "the kids" and "the grown-ups." The family encompasses two subgroups within the whole. With an only, there isn't such a ready-made division—parents and child are more blended. That has benefits, of course. It also contains the potential for the kind of enmeshment that can cause parents to turn their child into a mini-adult.

Live a life with your child *and* live your own separate, personal, private life with your spouse or partner. So many parents, I have found, feel uncomfortable about banishing their child from their activities. They think it's rude! Or perhaps damaging to the youngster's sense of security.

If you recognize such concerns in yourself, understand that *you're* the one who's worried that your son or daughter will feel excluded. It may be your projection, in other words, that this is such a hurtful thing; your child may not mind at all. But the more you stew and brood about leaving your youngster behind with the baby-sitter to go out to a movie or take a weekend vacation as a couple—or the more adamantly or indulgently you insist that he be allowed to "sit at the grown-ups' table"—the more that feeling of hurtful or resentful exclusion will be conveyed to your child. And then what was really a parents' problem becomes a child's problem.

Self-aware mothers and fathers can set up grown-up/child divisions comfortably, and later on we'll offer some thoughts on how to enjoy the special closeness that exists between parents and their only child, without overdoing it.

"WE INVITE HER FRIEND EVERYWHERE— I'VE GOT TO MAKE SURE SHE DOESN'T FEEL LONELY."

The mother of a now young-adult son remembers, "I couldn't stand it when I saw Jeremy playing by himself. I was always trying to hustle him over with other kids and always scheduling lots of things for him to do."

As an example, she recalls one outing at the beach, when Jeremy was a youngster. "He was happily amusing himself, concocting elaborate sand castles. He wasn't fretful, he was clearly having a perfectly good time. And I was sitting in my beach chair, watching him and getting more and more agitated. He was by himself for so long . . . didn't he want someone to play with? He *needed* someone to play with."

Jeremy's mother spotted a child down the beach who seemed to be about her son's age. "So I virtually dragged over this other boy and urged them to work on the sand castles together. Jeremy was annoyed. The other little boy was annoyed. They did not proceed to 'play well' together. But my whole feeling was: God forbid he should be lonely. Which, in fact, he wasn't."

Another parent says she was always extremely conscious of a need to get her son in an environment with other children when he was growing up, and often invited another youngster to join them when they went on outings or even on vacations. "And this sounds awful," she says, "but I have to admit that at times I caught myself not being sufficiently respectful of the other child as an individual but seeing him almost as a hired playmate.

"If I had voiced them out loud, my thoughts might have run:

'I brought you along to keep Michael company. What do you mean, you don't feel like playing?' I had to be very aware of this tendency. Interestingly, my oldest friend—she and I also are both only children—says that when we were little, she felt my mother treated her as the 'hired playmate' when she came to visit me."

The mother of an eleven-year-old girl says she has "pounced on a succession of little kids over the years because I was determined Eileen would have a best friend. At any particular time there was always one other little girl whom I tried to make virtually part of our lives."

Her daughter's friend-of-the-moment would be invited to family gatherings, to picnics, to plays, to sleepovers. Says this mother: "I don't regret this, because my kid had fun and a couple of these other children really did become good friends. But in retrospect, I think it would have been better for *me* if I had been able to lighten up a little about the whole thing. I was more emotionally invested in these friendships a lot of the time than Eileen was, and when some of them went sour, I took it harder than she did!"

IF YOU SEE YOURSELF IN THIS PICTURE . . .

Of course you want to encourage your child's friendships, and of course it's normal for every parent to want his child to be happy. As the parent of an only, though, you may find yourself assuming that solitary time must be avoided at all costs. Remember that there is pleasure in solitude, for children as well as adults, and only children—as we've said—often develop a fine and admirable capacity for being on their own. Take care not to send a message to your youngster that he should always be with others, and should want to be.

That message just might lead him to believe that there's something wrong with him if he often doesn't feel like having a playmate or if he enjoys being on his own. A young teenage girl, very astutely, was able to recognize her mother's projected feelings and separate them from her own. "It makes my mother so happy when I have a friend come home with me after school," says the girl. "She assumes I'm miserable if I'm just hanging out by myself in the afternoon. Actually, that's my favorite time of day and my favorite thing to do."

If you have genuine concerns that your child is feeling isolated or lonely, it's perfectly right to do a "happiness check." Watch and listen, and your youngster will communicate his feelings, if not in words, then through some kind of acting out—mopey periods that go on for too long, sleep or appetite changes, a slip in school performance, a long period of no friends or playmates around.

You can say to a school-age child, "Are you okay? Are things going on that are bothering you? I'm concerned." Perhaps together, then, you can come up with some ways he might become involved with new activities and a new set of potential friends. With a very young child, keep those play dates coming, and see if he might need a little help in learning playtime rules and compromises with his peers.

Only children generally have no more or less trouble making friends than do any others, and a solitary child is not necessarily feeling lonely. Take care not to project your own anxieties onto a situation that may not be at all troublesome to your youngster.

"HE'S SHY BECAUSE HE'S NOT AROUND OTHER KIDS."

Parents may make only-child excuses for their youngster's perceived inadequacies or shortcomings. The father and mother of one nine-year-old boy whose bed-wetting was a cause of deep distress to all three of them remained convinced that their son's difficulty persisted because he was an only child. That stirred up some deeply buried feelings of self-blame—the parents held on to a notion that they had done their son a disservice by not producing a larger family.

Another mother was plunged into despair over the midyear report that she received from her daughter's kindergarten teacher, which read: "This young child happens to be painfully shy, which affects her ability to communicate and makes it hard to judge the true potential of her cognitive growth." Although it went on to say that Jane was gradually gaining more confidence, both socially and academically, and that her teachers had seen enormous strides since the opening of school, Jane's mother decided her five-year-old daughter needed professional help and arranged for her to take a series of psychological tests.

In follow-up discussions with the psychologist—who had concluded that Jane was simply a retiring, slow-to-warm-up sort, and had seen no immediate need for therapy—the mother, quite agitated, reiterated her conviction that Jane was and would remain disadvantaged because she was an only child. So convinced was she that she told the psychologist she planned to investigate the possibility of adopting a second child—not a newborn, but an older child who could be a companion to her daughter.

IF YOU SEE YOURSELF IN THIS PICTURE . . .

Jane's mother's reactions were extreme, of course, but parents always tend to seek some way of rationalizing when things aren't going well with a child. They may say, "Well, his father had a learning disability, so therefore . . . ," or, "Well, it was a very difficult birth, so therefore . . ." It is not at all unusual—in fact, it can be normal and understandable—for a parent to use the "only" status as a ready-made explanation for a youngster's troubling behavior.

That tendency almost always ties in with any guilt the parent may retain about having just one child. In her heart, she may feel she should have provided her youngster with a brother or sister, or that there's some deficit in his life because he lacks a sibling. She may be inclined always to "make it up" to the child in various ways. And so she jumps to the conclusion that if anything goes wrong, it's because he's an only.

If your youngster is having some difficulties, take steps that seem appropriate. But prevent yourself from becoming painfully caught up in feelings that you did something wrong in not having more than one child, or that being an only justifies or explains any particular hurdle your son or daughter is navigating. To do so adds an unnecessary and really false burden to the situation. You can't successfully work your way out of it then, and chances are you'll have trouble giving your child the help and support he needs.

"LOTS OF ONLY KIDS ARE OBNOXIOUS/ SPOILED/CLINGY—I'M GOING TO BE SURE THAT DOESN'T HAPPEN WITH MY CHILD."

Everything we've talked about so far has concerned what parents, unintentionally, do that can perpetuate those disagreeable myths about only children. Here's one that represents what they do *not* do. As the flip side of making excuses for a child, some parents may feel such concern that their youngster *not* turn into the "typical" only that they become extremely vigilant about not coddling or overprotecting.

The mother of a college-age son, who raised him with little involvement from her divorced husband, remembers being perpetually on the alert for any signs that her only child was becoming a "mama's boy."

"Far from being too protective, I think I bent over backward in the other direction, so much that I may have made some foolish decisions," she says. "For example, I allowed Tyler to travel in

France one summer, when he was fifteen years old, accompanied by just one other boy—also an only child, as it happened. No adult supervision, no chaperons. I must have been out of my mind! Fortunately, it turned out okay."

Another parent recalls "an only child in my neighborhood when I was growing up, who was the most bossy, superior little brat I knew. Nobody liked this kid. I think it's common for onlies to feel they're king of the roost, because they get all that attention at home," she says. "I try to make sure Brian doesn't get too full of himself."

Brian, in fact, happens to be an unusually self-assured and gregarious little boy, who enjoys being in the limelight. But his mother is ever on the alert for signs of "brattiness." His kindergarten teacher told her, with a laugh, that Brian insisted on being the door holder for the rest of the kids as they returned to the classroom after recess, because he said he was the best door holder. Says Brian's mother: "I talked to him about this and told him he had to learn not to be so pushy, that he should give the other kids a chance to hold the door."

IF YOU SEE YOURSELF IN THIS PICTURE . . .

As an aware and thoughtful parent, trust your instincts, and grant appropriate freedoms at appropriate ages as your child grows toward a healthy independence. Take caution when caution is called for, let go when that's a good thing to do, and don't spend much energy worrying about over- or underprotecting your child.

It's good to remember, too, that your youngster, like all children, came into the world with his own special nature. He may be confident and outgoing, or an observer type who feels most comfortable taking a backseat, or somewhere in between. Brian's mother thought her son's "pushiness" might signal the "obnoxious brat" stereotype of the only child she detested.

More likely, Brian's take-charge behavior is a function of his unique personality and temperament, and as long as he's generally accepted by his peers, he's doing just fine.

"IF SHE SUCCEEDS, I SUCCEED— IF SHE FAILS, SO DO I."

To some extent, all parents, with any number of children, look to them to confirm their own sense of how well they're doing in life. Or they hope, perhaps unconsciously, that their children will triumph in a particular way they did not. That kind of investment in a youngster's accomplishments and achievements can be especially pronounced when there is just one child, and two parents look to that one to be the best of both of them.

One set of parents was so dismayed by their son's failure to attain top grades that they switched him from one private school to another almost on a yearly basis, searching for the one place they felt would "bring out his full potential." In truth, their son was and probably always would be an average, B-minus sort of student, a reality they could not accept because they felt themselves reduced in some way by his inability to do better. And their grazing among schools did little to bolster the boy's self-esteem.

Another couple had had their daughter, Annie, at the same time close friends also produced a daughter. As the years went on, Annie developed into a rather plain child and a fair student. She also had a charming, sweet-natured disposition and a fine sense of humor. The friends' daughter turned into a brilliant student who was also quite a beauty. Although this girl's parents were not in the least boastful or show-offy about their child, Annie's parents gradually broke off contact with them. Their sense of themselves was discomfited by what they perceived as their onetime friends' greater success as parents. And perhaps at some level they felt Annie reflected their own weaknesses.

Even in the smallest ways, a parent can invest much of herself in a child's accomplishments. The parent's sense of self soars or is diminished depending on the child.

That fact was powerfully demonstrated to me through a study my colleagues and I conducted. We sought to learn what mothers were thinking as they watched their toddlers go through a brief activity in the nursery: perhaps a youngster picked up a block and another child took it away from her, or a child joined a group of other youngsters. Some of these interactions lasted no longer than twenty seconds.

Then, for an hour and a half, we interviewed each mother, asking what was going through her mind about that twenty seconds. What became clear in those interviews was how much the parent was counting on the child to make up for some lack in her own life.

A mother said, "I was hoping she'd defend herself, but I didn't think she would. My brother always took my things and I couldn't do anything about it, and I was so surprised to see that she could handle herself." One mother watched as her son approached a table of children; the others all said, "Hi, Justin," and then Justin smiled and sat down with them. Later, that mother talked at length about how this thrilled her, because she herself had always been a shy outsider as a little girl.

IF YOU SEE YOURSELF IN THIS PICTURE . . .

Parents often entertain moment-to-moment hopes that a child will compensate for some limitation, weakness, or sadness they had or have about themselves. This is not a matter of a parent wishing, "I want him to become an astronaut/a pro football player/a pianist, because that's what I wanted to be myself and I never made it." Rather, it is an unconscious desire that "my child will be a little bolder/a little more talkative/a little friendlier than I was as a child, because if I had been like that I would have been a little happier."

With the only child, that process will be especially intense. It's deeply disturbing to a parent to see her child failing or not measuring up in just the way that she felt she failed. When a parent has two or three or four children, that investment is distributed differently. A mother will see fragments or moments in each child; if one is coming up short in an area in which she herself feels especially vulnerable, perhaps another youngster will shine in that particular way, and then she will feel reassured.

In some ways, of course, you want your child to be just like you. But like any parent, you will probably have other aspects of your nature or your life that you hope your child does not duplicate. It's a normal and manageable human instinct. Just do be conscious of tendencies to invest too much of your own sense of self in what's happening with your child, and of your need to have your youngster "do better" than you did in one way or another.

· 7 ·

The Family Triangles, Good and Bad

HOW TO FORGE A HEALTHY THREESOME

The minute your child is born, you, your spouse, and your baby form a triangle. Where there were two, suddenly there are three. During the active parenting years, up until the time your child perhaps leaves home for college, how well that triangle "works" will have an effect on how comfortably, happily, and healthily you all live together—and how successfully your child embarks finally on an independent life.

Psychologists use the term "triangulation" to refer to the push-and-pull currents that flow among three people. Within a mother/father/child threesome, those currents are formed by several factors and include these realities:

- *Triangulation is a normal,* organic, ongoing process that is part of how a child develops and grows into an adult.

- *Your child will* **need** *one parent more* or in different ways at different stages in her development.

- *Mother, father, and child,* consciously or unconsciously, will over time enter into ever-shifting, two-versus-one alignments.

- *You and your spouse* may very likely come at the business of raising a child from different perspectives.

- *Triangulation happens in all families,* no matter how many children there are. Keeping it a healthy process can be especially tricky for the parents of an only child.

In this chapter, we'll offer ideas on how to keep the triangle functioning well, and we'll talk about signs that indicate it may be running into trouble—how triangulation can turn from a positive to a negative.

Two mothers who shared their child-raising experiences and thoughts for this book told us anecdotes that, I believe, illustrate very well some typical ways normal parent/parent/child triangulation operates and that suggest some of the special challenges for the only-child family. Here are their stories:

Lydia is the mother of a three-year-old daughter, Devon. Lydia works as a physician's receptionist during the hours that Devon is in preschool, and picks her daughter up in the afternoon. Just recently, she says, "the honeymoon between Devon and me has most definitely ended! Whereas previously I could do no wrong, now there's no one as perfect as Daddy, and I'm the wicked witch."

When Devon's father arrives home in the evening, "she's all over him, and I am often literally pushed out of the way. Gary and I mostly get a kick out of this, and Gary tells me, 'Well, you were king for a while, now I'm king. No doubt your star will rise again!' And I do know that this is a phase she's going through, but I still can get very irked and irritated sometimes by both of them. All this rejection from this little kid doesn't feel nice! And then I think I do really have a better idea than he does about how to handle certain situations, because I spend more time with her."

Lydia and her husband have been able to talk over her feelings about what's going on, and have come up with some ways to bring more balance into the picture.

"Sometimes lately I'll take off early on a Saturday and spend the whole day at my sister's, and we just relax and have some laughs," she says. "And then Gary gets the full brunt of being the parent, and I think that's been eye-opening for him. He can't always be the good guy—he has to get into saying no and disciplining. And he has more understanding of what goes on during my day with her."

Lydia and her husband, she says, have also made a point of "getting a baby-sitter and going out more as just the two of us. Just for an early dinner or a movie. We say that for at least an hour we will talk about anything *except* Devon."

Annette, the mother of nine-year-old Peter, says, "It's easy to get into triangle situations when you have an only child, and some of these, I think, are positive alignments. Peter and I like to do certain things together, for instance. We both love playing board games—once we got past the age of Candyland and Chutes & Ladders, which I couldn't bear! We both like card games. All of which my husband doesn't especially enjoy. Wally doesn't even know how to hold the cards, forget about shuffling!"

They rib each other about their differences, says Annette, in a way that seems to feel comfortable to everybody. "Peter and I joke about how Dad is such a klutz, and that's affectionate. And they make fun of me in little ways—how I'm always losing my glasses, how I always have to go to the bathroom just as we're leaving the house. Then, Wally and Peter have their own things they do together, like fishing, and their guy things, like belching contests. Although now Wally is trying to discontinue the belching contests—having perfected the art, stop already!"

What sometimes concerns this mother is a different kind of teaming up that tends to happen in her household. Because an only child spends so much time in the exclusive company of Mom and Dad, he picks up on a lot of what's going on with each of them. And because there's no one else around to talk to or share those perceptions with, he's more likely than his siblinged peers to make adult-style observations to one parent about the other.

"There's a kind of parent/kid alignment I see going on among us sometimes that I think is not so healthy," Annette explains. "Wally tends to get moody and prickly in the evenings, for example. And Peter will look over at me and roll his eyes—sort of a 'There goes Daddy again' look—and this bothers me. If he had a brother or sister around, maybe they'd be rolling their eyes at each other, which would be okay. And when Peter does that with me, it puts pressure on me, because I'd like to roll my eyes right back and say, 'Yeah, there he goes again!' As the mother and the parent, I think I should stay on the adult side of the alignment, although my sympathies are with the kid!"

One evening, Annette took her son aside and said, "You know, Dad gets a little tired by the end of the day, and that can make him act cranky sometimes." Later, she let her husband know that even if he's feeling stressed, she and Peter both would like it if he tried not to let his moodiness intrude on their family time.

Both these mothers, with a high degree of self-awareness, astutely recognized and described some three-way currents playing out in their families. (They also instinctively came up with some good ways to keep the triangle balanced, and we'll talk more about that later on.)

These small conflicts of loyalty, shifts in allegiance, pairings-up, and all the other elements of triangulation are going on all day long. A lot of the time, they're happening "behind the scenes," at a level that we're not all that aware of. Parents who have their wits about them—in my experience, that means first and foremost maintaining a clear understanding of themselves as adults and of their child as a child—know how to "go with the flow."

They perceive when Mother should be a little to the foreground and when Father should be more front and center; when to allow the child the indulgence of saying, "I only want Daddy," and when to say, "You know, you're really hurting my feelings, cut it out"; when to encourage father/child and mother/child twosomes, and when to devote a little more attention to the father/mother twosome.

In the only-child family, keeping that triangulation process healthy can be especially challenging. Excluding the child from something pleasant going on in the parents' lives may seem hard to do, while including the child in something not so pleasant may be tempting. It's easier for a mother or father to feel the child's attempts to include or exclude one or the other of them as more satisfying, more hurtful, or in some other way more meaningful than typically would the parent of two or three children.

And on the other side of the equation, that only youngster doesn't have the avenue of siblings as a means of stepping out of the triangle from time to time. He can't say, in effect, "There's mother, there's father, but there's my brother and sister, and I think I'll go to them for a while now."

Lydia's and Annette's observations underscore the two elements that I believe are critical in making sure that triangulation remains positive: The adults must understand that their child is little and is growing up, and must remember to treat him as a growing child and not as an adult. And the adults must have a separate relationship, one that is based on mutual respect for each other as a parent, and that has to do with the feelings and activities they share as grown-ups and that do not involve their child.

Before we suggest some specific ways you can ensure that those elements are well and thriving, I think it will be helpful to talk a little about what part triangulation plays in how a child develops psychologically. (To explain these ages and stages, it's easiest to present them within the context of the intact two-parent/one-child family. But with variations, the same needs and behaviors are going on if you're a divorced parent raising your child singly or with joint custody, if you are a father who is the primary caregiver of your child, or if you live in a home with other caregiving adults who are involved with your child.)

AGES AND STAGES: HOW TRIANGULATION WORKS TO HELP YOUR CHILD GROW

Many investigators, myself included, believe that there is a built-in, biologically determined purpose to the triad and the triangulation that results from it. Even within a family that includes several children, the goal for each child is the same, if he is eventually to become an adult ready to have his own family.

Broadly stated, that goal is to become psychologically independent of his parent or parents (that may, again, be grandmother, aunt, or whoever else is the primary caregiver).

Here's how it works:

BABYHOOD: THE BLISSFUL TWOSOME

During the first few months or perhaps the first year in his life, the child is primarily involved in a dyad—an intense one-on-one relationship with his mother. Other people are there, of course, but he doesn't yet have the capacity to handle a variety of relationships. Until he gets his bearings, he needs that deeply loving, intimate, all-accepting connection with a primary person. All is well.

Starting sometime around seven or eight months and building cumulatively all through toddlerhood, things change. His adoring mom now is saying, "No, don't pull my glasses off," "No fingers in my hair," "Stay away from that light plug," "No throwing food on the floor" . . . and suddenly Mom doesn't look as good as she used to! The child has no understanding, really, of what's going on; Mother, who was all nurturing and loving, is acting in ways that don't make sense and that he doesn't like. The honeymoon is over.

TODDLERHOOD: INVESTING IN A THIRD PARTY

Once the child sees Mother as, at least a lot of the time, a prohibitor, he starts feeling angry toward her. Then Father starts to come into focus; suddenly he's looking very good, and that can be an important impetus to the beginning of triangulation. Early triangulation in part is about the child's angry feelings and his wish to move away from the parent he's feeling angry about by investing in somebody else.

In the old traditional family setup, in which Mother and child were home together all day and Father arrived back from work in the evening, Daddy was a breath of fresh air—in a sense, his youngster was saying, "Yay, Daddy's home! He's new and different and fun. I think I'll go to Daddy."

These early efforts to become involved with a third person set up for the child a model or a pathway for a constant shifting back and forth that will continue throughout childhood. It's a pathway that's very useful during the next phase of his development, when things become much more complex.

THE OEDIPAL PERIOD: DEALING WITH SCARY FEELINGS

For the toddler, switching allegiance to another parent is mainly a matter of "Who's going to be nicer to me right now?" Starting around the age of four or five, triangulation becomes a more complicated business, because it now involves sexual elements, grandiose notions, and ideas of gender.

The little boy thinks he can marry Mom and sees himself as a rival of Dad. The little girl thinks she'd make a much better wife for Dad than Mom is (because Mom is so grumpy). Those are upsetting feelings for that youngster, which he or she deals with by engaging in a great deal of back-and-forth between parents. For the little girl, the feelings might be described as: "I love Daddy and I don't love Mommy. But this is scary. So I really do love Mommy and I'm going to cling to her (so Mommy won't know I really love Daddy)." For the little boy, the dynamic is reversed.

Triangulation now helps the youngster handle those perhaps frightening feelings and in time resolve them, which may take several years of going back and forth. By the end of the oedipal period, the child realizes and feels comfortable with the notion that his mom and dad have a private life with each other that doesn't include him.

LATENCY: GOING ABOUT HIS BUSINESS

When all has gone well during that earlier stage of triangulation, the child puts to rest his grandiose wishes to take over his parent's role and enjoys several years in which he uses his solid grasp of himself *as a child* to get on with the business of doing what a child does. During the ages of roughly seven to eleven, his fantasy life preoccupies him less. He's ready to focus his attentions on going to school and learning and involving himself in the world of his peers.

He's gearing up for the next stage of development.

ADOLESCENCE: GETTING READY TO MOVE ON

Teenagers, of course, are notorious for their rebellions against parents, who suddenly may not be able to do anything right. But again, a great deal of shifting back and forth may be going on as that youngster starts to become aware of his own sexual identity and explore the possibilities of love relationships outside his family.

A boy whose parents are divorced and who has been living contentedly with his mother and visiting Dad on weekends, for example, may suddenly express a fervent wish to go and live with his father. A girl who has happily been spending weekends with her father for years may suddenly decide she doesn't want to do that anymore unless she can bring a friend along. In these and other ways, triangulation during the adolescent years may have to do with which parent, through no particular actions on his or her own part, helps the child feel temporarily more comfortable with his own sexual identity as he moves forward into young adulthood.

This brief summary of how a child typically develops psychologically shows that triangulation is not only an inevitable but also a useful force in the process. Although these feelings and behaviors may sound like the stuff of high drama ("I hate Mommy, I'm going to marry Daddy," and so on), they happen for the child on a preconscious level. This idea of which parent the child wants is part of the child's inner life, and it may shift by the day or the hour.

You can ride with those shifts and have a great time with your child along the way, if you keep in mind some basic rules for healthy triangulation.

Here is what I consider most important:

KNOW SOMETHING ABOUT YOUR CHILD'S AGES AND STAGES

You need not be overly analytical. You need not become an expert in child development. You need not know more, really, than the rough outline we've just described, in order to appreciate a little of what's probably going on in the inner life of your child at age two or five or eleven.

That awareness, coupled with your good sense and your love for your youngster, will help you to know when to step in or step back. It will help you to "not take it personally," to see the ways in which you are separate from your child, and to understand when, as Devon's mother said, your child is going through a phase. That alone goes a long way toward keeping the triangle working well.

REMEMBER THAT THREE FAMILY MEMBERS DON'T ALWAYS GET THREE EQUAL VOTES

The triangle doesn't contain three equal partners. It's so important for the parents of an only child to *not* make the child always "one of us." When she is treated as an equal, she may have an especially difficult time coming to understand that there's something about Mother and Father that's different from her—that they have a sexual relationship, a love relationship, a working-to-pay-the-bills relationship, and a whole lot else that she does not have.

A mother and father were talking about their plans for a ten-day vacation trip the family would take during their daughter's spring break at school. "Steve and I really wanted to drive along the Gulf Coast," said the mother, "but Melissa insisted on Key West, so I guess that's what we'll do." Melissa is nine. That child was allowed *more* than an equal vote; her minority-of-one opinion carried the day!

It is perfectly all right, of course, to ask for your child's input on family decisions and to consider her preferences. It is even sometimes all right to allow her an equal vote in a matter up for discussion, depending on what's at stake and on whether or not you feel it's appropriate for her ideas to carry the same weight as yours. Just remember who's in charge.

In my practice, I see many modern-day parents of only children working very hard at being "good" mothers and "good" fathers. They try always to make the child feel central, treating him as an equal, letting him make decisions that really should be left to the grown-ups. They hang on the child's every word.

And what I see, too, is that many of those doted-on young-sters have a hard time entering larger situations with other children. Privileged and exalted in their own homes, they can't tolerate the shift in their position in the world and find it difficult being just one of the gang in the classroom. They may not engage with other children appropriately but look at them as rivals.

When parents are not the real authorities in the home, they, in effect, put pressure on the child. Children really do desperately want to feel that there is someone greater than they are, someone who lets them know the way the world goes! When they are elevated to adult equal, they may experience a great deal of anxiety—first, they have too much control, and second, there is no one to protect them when they are frightened.

Child psychiatrist Stanley Turecki writes that the ideal parent/child relationship contains benign adult leaders and junior collaborators. I like that idea that the family functions best as neither a dictatorship nor a democracy. Everyone can speak his piece, but the final word rests with the grown-ups.

YOU HAVE THE RIGHT TO PRIVACY— SO DOES YOUR CHILD

The mother of a five-year-old girl says she finally "resorted to getting the ancient, nonfunctioning lock on our bedroom door repaired, so my husband and I can let Erica know we really do want her to stay out of our room sometimes. She is not happy about this, but it's the only way to keep her out." Erica, says her mother, also likes to sit on the bathroom chair and talk while her mom is showering, and lately this mother has taken to locking the bathroom door too.

Erica's mother has the right idea: she is entitled to privacy at times. But the means she's used to convey that message to her child—locked doors—is extreme and could be seen by Erica as visible proof that she's being shut out of her parents' lives. I would guess the measure would not have become necessary if these parents had in small ways conveyed all along—from Erica's toddlerhood on—the notion that everybody in the family wants and needs some "space," times or places that are not going to be shared.

Here's what to remember:

- **Start with the idea** that you are entitled to a private life. Indeed, insisting on that privacy is good not only for you but for your youngster too.

- **Find your own ways** to get that message across without seeming angry or exclusionary or resorting to extreme measures. One set of parents decided that it suited them to keep one room, their bedroom, in their large apartment off-limits to their child. When their little boy reached toddler age, they installed a folding child's gate across their bedroom door. The youngster accepted this barrier without protest, and now, many years later, with the gate long gone, still doesn't go into his parents' room unless he's invited.

- **Respect your child's privacy.** Around age four or five, most children become suddenly modest about their bodies and bodily functions. Be sensitive to those changes in your child's attitude. Over the years, she probably will make very clear, too, that she wants her room to be off-limits for a while or that in other ways she needs private time and space.

BREAK UP THE THREESOME OCCASIONALLY BY TAKING "GROWN-UPS-ONLY TIME"

Without question, it takes more effort to enforce adult/child distinctions in the only-child household. Two parents going out to a movie on a Friday evening can feel miserable about leaving their child behind. They worry that he's going to be lonely.

They think they're being unfriendly. And when they emanate those unhappy feelings, their child probably *is* going to feel hurt and gloomy and abandoned. With two or three children, a child's attitude is more likely to be: "Good, Mom and Dad are going out. Maybe we can get the baby-sitter to let us stay up late."

Taking time for yourself as a couple—to go on an outing, to have a grown-ups-only conversation—is not being unfriendly and is not exclusionary to your child. On the contrary, it gives him critical opportunities to experience the adult/child distinction and to recognize that the two grown-ups he's so attached to have a special relationship that doesn't have to do with him.

The trick is to separate your child from yourself without sounding punitive. You might, for example, say:

"Mom and Dad haven't had a chance to talk all day. We're just going to sit here and chat. This is boring for you, so why don't you go in your room and play. Later, we'll play a game together."

Or: "Honey, we're talking right now, and we don't want to be interrupted for a while. This is a good time for you to do some coloring in your book."

Or: "We're going out to dinner tomorrow evening, and you'll be staying home. What should we set up for you to do? Should we call Sarah and see if she can come over to play?"

BREAK UP THE THREESOME OCCASIONALLY BY SPENDING ONE-ON-ONE TIME WITH YOUR CHILD

Just as Mom and Dad need their twosome times, it's healthy for mother and child and father and child to step out of the triangle on occasion.

A father and his seven-year-old daughter enjoy weekend afternoons exploring in their neighborhood and playing "tell that story," a little game they invented and that has evolved over the years. "It started when Annie was about four and we were on our way to the playground one Saturday," he says. "We passed a building that had a big splatter of paint on one wall, and I asked Annie what she thought had happened there. She said she thought a painter dropped a bucket of paint. I said I didn't see how you could 'drop' a bucket on a wall. Then we started going back and forth with different versions of how the paint got there, and we got sillier and more fanciful as we went along. That evening when she was going to bed, she said, 'Tell that story about the paint again, Daddy.'"

Annie and her dad have had a lot of creative fun going for their walks and making up their stories, many of which, says this father, led to interesting discussions on a variety of topics. Sometimes Annie's father felt her stories opened a little window into what she was thinking and feeling about events in her life; once, for example, a made-up tale about a little girl who couldn't find her way home from school might have been her way of airing anxieties she was having about her first days in kindergarten.

This dad is a whimsical and inventive man with a special knack for tuning in to his young child in this imaginative way. It's a knack his wife apparently doesn't share. "Sometimes I got the feeling that Marie was resentful of Annie and me having such a good time just hanging out together and doing all this talking," he says. "Finally, my wife and I had a talk about it, and she said she did feel a little jealous. I told her she was the unrivaled expert on overseeing homework, throwing fantastic kid birthday parties, making Halloween costumes, and a hundred other things."

It is common, I have found, for one adult in a family of three to feel miffed or hurt when his partner and his child are having a good time without him. The mother of a nine-year-old says she and her son, Corin, are "movie freaks who see everything that comes along. Marty [her husband] doesn't like going to movies, and that's okay. But sometimes it can feel uncomfortable when Corin and I will have spent a Saturday together and had this really nifty time, and when we get home there's a sense that Daddy has been kind of left out of things. And Marty, I feel, tries to compensate by being excessively nice to Corin and insisting they play games or something."

It is good and natural for your only child to enjoy times in the exclusive company of one or another parent. If you or your partner have hurt or left-out feelings, remember this:

- *Your child will almost surely* go back and forth over the years in feeling one parent or the other is her current "favorite." Don't pressure her to bestow equally affectionate attentions on both her parents all the time.

- *You and your partner almost inevitably* bring different individual strengths or talents to the business of child raising. Maybe Dad is a good storyteller and Mom is a good homework helper. Play to those strengths, and don't feel you must be all things to your youngster.

- *It really is healthy for your child* if the intensity of the threesome is diffused from time to time, and for each parent/child pair to enjoy some "hanging-out-together," one-on-one times.

It is an accepted value in our society that girls will look to mothers and boys will look to fathers for their earliest lessons in gender identification. But it is important, too, for a youngster to enjoy a warm relationship with an opposite-sex parent or other adult. A girl's sense of femininity evolves vis-à-vis her father, and a boy learns a great deal about being around women from his relationship with his mother.

Your healthily growing child, then, will most likely favor one or the other of his parents at different times for different reasons. You'll keep the triangle working well when you accept those shifts and take care that the grown-ups remain the grown-ups, that the child remains the child, and that twosomes have opportunities to thrive.

DIFFERENT PARENTING STYLES: HOW THEY AFFECT TRIANGLES

The other primary factor, mentioned at the beginning of this chapter, that influences the currents of triangulation has to do with something else entirely: You and your spouse may come at the business of raising a child from very different perspectives. Your own family history, whether you're a man or a woman, the amount and nature of the time each of you spends with your youngster—these and other realities can produce different parenting styles, and those, in turn, have a lot to do with what goes on in the triangle.

Here is a scene that I think vividly demonstrates how fathers and mothers can sometimes be on opposite sides of the parenting fence:

Four sets of parents, all good friends, were having dinner together, minus their kids. Jim and Merrill, father and mother of eight-year-old Megan, suddenly became involved in a spirited discussion over an incident concerning their daughter. Megan had just started attending a summer day camp, and things apparently were off to a bumpy start. Although she had had a fine time at the same camp the previous year, friendships and alliances had shifted, and Megan's once best friend, Kathryn, was now her enemy. The two girls had had a big blowup one afternoon, and when Megan told her mother she wanted to stay home from camp the following day, Merrill was sympathetic and allowed her to "take some time off." Jim didn't approve and thought Merrill was being a wimp.

"The two kids had a little falling-out, and Merrill thinks it's the end of the world," said Jim. "Actually, *worse* than the end of the world. I could call Merrill at work and say World War III is probably going to start next week, and she'd say, 'Is that right? But you know, Megan was so upset when Kathryn said that to her. . . .'" Jim was smiling as he talked, poking a little good-natured fun—he thought—at his wife.

"She *was* very upset," said Merrill, indignantly. "The next morning she was all teary and said her stomach hurt, and I thought there was nothing wrong with letting her take a cooling-off day. But Jim thinks I'm making a big deal out of nothing and giving in to Megan."

Jim, now getting a little heated: "Kids have to learn how to fight their own battles. This kind of thing happens a lot with Megan. She has to grow a thicker skin. Not let these run-ins with other kids bother her so much. That's not going to happen if she removes herself from the fray."

Merrill: "I think *you're* the one who's making a big deal out of this. Missing one day is not backing away from a problem. And anyway, this does *not* happen a lot. Megan generally gets along very well with other kids."

One of the other mothers jumped in. "That's right, she does," she said to Jim, good-naturedly but with a hint of a bite in her voice. "But you probably don't see her interacting very much because you probably don't do the play dates and the birthday parties and the school trips. Am I right?"

"Interacting! I love that word!" said this woman's husband, in a tone that indicated he didn't love it at all. "This is something *we* get into all the time about the kids," he added to the group at large. "We both work and we're both involved with the kids, but Grace pulls out that I-do-it-all argument, and that's supposed to give her the last word."

Merrill, sounding really annoyed: "I am not saying that I do it all or that Jim isn't involved, but I am saying that I do most of it and I certainly have spent more time than he has observing her around other children."

"You men come swooping in with some major, vague, tough-talk sort of statement," said husband number two's wife, "like 'Megan has to get a thicker skin,' or, 'You have to take a tougher line.' And usually you're completely oblivious to all the little details surrounding some incident."

"That's exactly the point!" said Merrill.

The host abruptly suggested that everybody move out to the backyard for iced tea.

HE SAYS, SHE SAYS: HOW MEN AND WOMEN ACT AS PARENTS

The animated exchange above reveals an often overlooked parenting fact of life—a mother and a father can be convinced that each knows best what's right for their child. Having different opinions is normal, and it's by no means a bad thing. (In fact, as we'll see later, when Mom and Dad are always, unwaveringly, of one mind, the triangle loses flexibility in ways that can feel overpowering or stultifying to their child.) But when different parenting styles and attitudes are pervasive or deep-rooted or lead to regular arguments, good, healthy, positive triangulation can turn into a negative. In this section, we'll look at some possible reasons you and your spouse may be on different wavelengths.

The fact that men and women often don't come at the matter of child raising in the same way shouldn't be surprising. If men are from Mars and women are from Venus regarding many of life's experiences, communications, and expectations, as popular books and magazine articles keep telling us, why should it be any different when it comes to how they act as parents?

In general:

MOTHERS STILL DO MOST OF THE HANDS-ON CHILD CARE; FATHERS ARE STILL "HELPING OUT"

Although 1990s fathers do change diapers, throw in a load of wash, and attend teacher conferences with more regularity than most of their fathers did, mothers—whether they hold down jobs outside the home or not—are still the main child care providers in the home. According to recent Census Bureau figures, four-fifths of working wives with husbands were the primary caretakers of children under age five. And men's involvement in child care declines as children grow older—fathers were the main caregivers for only 8 percent of children aged five to fourteen.

Even when fathers are participants and think they're fully engaged with their wives in bringing up the child, they still tend to be on the periphery of the daily nitty-gritty.

For his book *Why Parents Disagree*, child psychologist Ron Taffel asked a father and a mother, the parents of two children, to keep separate lists of what chores and activities each did around the home in the course of a typical late afternoon and evening, a matter of about six or seven hours. This young couple, before preparing their lists, considered themselves thoroughly "modern" parents, with if not quite a fifty-fifty sharing of parenting chores, something like a sixty (her)–forty (him) division of labor. They were shaken, says Taffel, to see written down in black and white just what did go on in the household on an average evening.

The father's list contained twelve items, including "put dishes in dishwasher," "discuss homework," "organize myself for making breakfast the next morning."

The mother's list ran to forty-six items. Here are some of them: "make about twenty phone calls as class mother to plan fourth-grade square dance," "wrap baby-sitter's Christmas gift," "check Eric's first-grade project," "remind Eric to pack his bag for sleep-over," "complete permission form so Chloe can attend class trip," and so on, in what Taffel calls a typical "Mom's Endless List."

MOTHERS SOMETIMES FEEL THEY CAN "DO IT BETTER"; FATHERS SAY THEY SOMETIMES FEEL PUSHED ASIDE

No doubt because they do so deeply engage themselves in "all the little details," as that mother said, and because they do maintain the Endless List, mothers tend to feel that they, better than their spouses, can get done what needs doing faster, more accurately, and with greater understanding of "what's really going on." I have heard many a father complain, "My wife says she wants me to get more involved with our child, but then she'll tell me that I'm not doing something right, or she'll jump in and do it first or take over anyway."

MOTHERS SPEND MORE TIME THAN FATHERS DO OBSERVING THEIR CHILD IN THE COMPANY OF OTHER CHILDREN

As that dinner guest pointed out, usually it *is* the mothers who do most of the shepherding of kids to and from the play dates and the birthday parties, who volunteer to be parent chaperons on the second-grade outing to the zoo.

They do have more opportunities to see that most toddlers aren't happy about sharing toys, and most six-year-old girls pair off in intense friendships, and most eight-year-old boys like superheroes. And thus they can perhaps more accurately gauge how their own child measures up in terms of "age-appropriate" behavior.

"WHEN I WAS A KID . . .": PAST SCENARIOS IN THE PRESENT TENSE

Because of the kinds and amounts of parenting time each expends, because of the way men and women have been socialized, you and your spouse, then, may approach the matter of what a parent should be like from different perspectives. Add to that your own individual *ghosts of the past,* and child-rearing differences that affect how the triangle is working are inevitable.

As we saw in an earlier chapter, how you were brought up

plays a powerful role in the way you consciously or unconsciously go about creating your own family. If you grew up in a happy home and like what your parents did, you want to repeat your own history. Whether you're fully aware of it or not, you'll tend to repeat the past if you maintain the attitude that "it worked for me, it will work for my kid," or, "this is what parents are like because this is how my parents were." Others, who had consistently unhappy times with their own parents and are determined not to make the same mistakes, will try to repair the past. All those ghosts of the past can become part of the triangle in small or more significant ways that divide a mother and father:

"My husband and I have ongoing food battles," says the mother of a seven-year-old. "Frank is of the old 'eat your vegetables, no dessert until you've cleaned your plate' school, just like his mother. Whereas I figure, what's the harm in a Twinkie lunch now and then?"

"Bill and I each went to single-sex Catholic schools from kindergarten through high school," says another mother. "He hated it, I loved it. Those places were a spiritual, nourishing environment for me, and I want our daughter to have the same experience, but Bill is adamantly opposed to anything except public school for her. Fortunately, we still have two years before she starts school to work this out!"

THE MAN/WOMAN EQUATION: HOW TO GET MORE IN SYNC

If you recognize yourself or your spouse in some of the "what men do/what women do" generalizations we described—or if you're aware that a lot of the time you're walking around feeling mildly annoyed or downright seething about who does what and when—consider how you might bring about some adjustments. Here are a few suggestions:

IMPROVE JOINT PARTICIPATION,
IF IT NEEDS IMPROVING

If your household runs by Mom's Endless List, sit down with your spouse and see what can be done to work out a more equitable division of chores and responsibilities. If your spouse doesn't "get it" and is convinced he's pulling his weight in child care matters, and you're equally convinced he's not, suggest you both try the "write down what you did today" exercise. Then—in a friendly manner and the spirit of cooperation—talk over how you might redistribute tasks.

RELINQUISH SOME CONTROL, IF YOU
RECOGNIZE YOU'VE BEEN HOLDING
ON TO MOST OF IT

If you're a mother who's used to being "in charge," let Dad do things his way sometimes and see what happens. Probably nothing terrible—there's more than one way to give a child a bath. Or, if your child is always coming to you with a problem, encourage him sometimes to seek out his other parent. And try not to play intermediary. Your child needs an ongoing relationship with each of his parents, together and individually.

SWITCH ROLES SOMETIMES

If Mom always makes the play date arrangements and does the birthday party drop-offs and pickups, Dad might take over occasionally. It really is helpful for a parent who doesn't often see his child among peers to get a sense of how children act in groups.

CONSIDER EACH OTHER'S POINT OF VIEW

Mom regularly thinks Dad needs to do more negotiating with their child in small daily matters; Dad regularly thinks Mom needs to take a tougher line or stop "spoiling" their child. Probably each point has some validity, and what's best for their child may be somewhere in the middle. The most effective parenting decisions both respect the child's perspective or feelings *and* promote commitment to the grown-ups' standards of behavior.

WHEN PARENTING DIFFERENCES START TO CAUSE TRIANGULATION TROUBLE

Given the different emotions and histories you and your spouse may bring to the family triangle, it's unlikely that you'll always be in parental alliance. That's normal. You and your spouse are *not always going to agree* about what's good for your child.

You think, for example, that removing privileges—no Nintendo for two days—is the most effective way to let your child know that something she's doing is wrong; your spouse believes that kind of "punishment" doesn't work and wants to reason things out with the youngster. You are badgering your child to get out his bike or Rollerblades, because it drives you batty to see him lounging around inside on a beautiful Saturday afternoon; your spouse has no problem with this. You want your "no candy" rule to apply at all times; your spouse thinks you should make an exception while visiting the grandparents, who enjoy indulging your child with goodies.

If, as ideally is the case, each of you is lovingly and consistently engaged with your youngster—if one parent does not, out of inertia or lack of confidence, abdicate child-raising decisions to the other—then almost inevitably there will be times when you do not present yourselves as a parental united front.

Your child can accept the fact that sometimes Mom and Dad have different ideas. Too impenetrable a parenting block, in fact, can be oppressive to a child. When she sees Mom and Dad as an unwavering, monolithic unit—always in agreement, always speaking as one voice—she can feel like the odd person out, overwhelmed, outnumbered, outmaneuvered.

The mother of an only child, who herself grew up an only, remembers wishing sometimes that she had a sibling, "just so there'd be another one of my species in the house!" she says. "I remember often feeling that, with my parents, it was always 'two against one.' They never seemed to disagree on anything, especially anything having to do with me. I must admit that I used to envy kids who had a brother or sister to be on their side."

If some disagreement is inevitable and normal—and even good for a child, who really does benefit from being able to connect to two different parents in different ways—persistent and pervasive "parenting incompatibilities" between a mother and a father are damaging to the triangle.

A child needs to feel anchored and safe at home in order to expend his young energies on learning what he needs to learn about the bigger world outside. He feels safest when Mom and Dad, most of the time, are able to work together as the grownups in charge of the triangle. Indeed, much research shows that parents who are on the same wavelength and who feel supported by each other are *better parents*—more relaxed, responsive, and patient with their children. It makes sense. If you know that your mate backs you up and generally thinks you're doing a good job as a mother or as a father, you will feel more confident and more inclined to keep right on trying to do a good job.

Conversely, when his mother and father have a lot of trouble acting as a coordinated "parenting team," a child can't feel anchored and safe. And those uncomfortable feelings can take their toll. One study showed that children whose mothers and fathers exhibited greatly differing child-rearing attitudes had the worst grades. Another study, of young boys, connected parents' persistent wrangling and disagreement with a youngster's being more likely to hurt other children, break things, or be disobedient.

Let's explore some ways the triangle can run into trouble.

HOME-FRONT BATTLEGROUNDS:
WHEN PARENTS FIGHT

Most children hate it when their parents fight. Only children hate it *and* they can feel terribly alone and abandoned, with no one with whom to share their feelings of fear.

Seventeen-year-old Renee remembers this scene: "When I was about five, my folks got into a huge blowup one day about who should be the one to close the windows because it was raining. And usually they never had fights. I went into my room and crawled under my desk. I sat there thinking if I had never been born this wouldn't have happened."

Renee's mother remembers that afternoon too. "It's true that Rick and I never got into noisy, shouting fights like this one was. And the argument popped up really because of some other gripe I had at the time toward Rick, not because of the rain and the windows. But I walked into Renee's room later and saw that little white face under the desk, and it felt as if I had slapped her."

Interestingly, this mother remembered back to her own childhood and how she handled things when she heard her parents arguing. "When my mother and dad got into a fight, my brother and I would hang out in our bedroom. We each had little wads of Silly Putty, and we'd lie on our beds and have a contest to see who could throw the Silly Putty up closest to the ceiling without touching it—you hit the ceiling, you lost! So we'd hear this yelling going on downstairs, and he and I would have our contest and not talk much, but it felt so good to be together. And that afternoon with Renee, I remembered that and felt sad that she had to hang out all alone until the battle was over."

Siblings can be empathic links and a comfort to each other at such times—or, as discussed previously, marital fighting sometimes actually *increases* hostility or discord between siblings. In any case, because she is an only child, your youngster is likely to be acutely sensitive to and upset by fights between you and your spouse. The scariest parental fights involve heated arguments, raised voices, name calling, or any physical displays of anger.

Your child will be especially distressed if she's aware that the fight is about a child-raising issue—because she's the only child around, she "knows" she is guilty and to blame. (And like Renee, young children in particular may feel they're to blame even if the dispute has nothing to do with them.)

As grown-ups, however, we all know that the occasional fight is part of life, because anger is part of life. And most children are relatively resilient individuals who, even though they don't like it while it's going on, will not suffer from normal levels of anger in the home. In fact, a youngster gets a critical, real-life learning opportunity when she sees, in her own home, that people who love each other have differences and conflicts, and that they can work them out and solve problems together.

It is how parents handle fights that makes the difference in how successfully children deal with their own feelings about the whole thing.

FIGHTING THE GOOD FIGHT: FIVE STEPS TO CONFLICT MANAGEMENT

Much research in family dynamics, and my own professional experience in working with many sets of parents, suggests these rules for handling angry conflicts:

- *Don't sit on your anger toward your spouse.* Your child will know what's going on if you're giving each other the silent treatment. Nonverbal expressions of anger are recognizable—and upsetting—to children. They also teach a child that uncomfortable feelings should be stifled, and that's not healthy.

- *Don't let anger get out of hand.* Children become *more* distressed the *more* intensely anger between their parents is expressed. Physical aggression is the most upsetting.

- *Learn to give each other cues.* Many parents can successfully use a signal or code word, like "talk later," to diffuse angry tension and postpone a heated discussion until a time their child is not present.

- *Resolve your fight.* Ideally, an argument is never just a sounding off with a lot of complaints and grievances, but a process that leads toward a conclusion of differences. And your child will *know* when you and your spouse reach a real resolution—one that involves genuine apology or committed compromise and the restoration of "friendly relations"—even if that happens sometime after the fight and out of her earshot. Vent your spleen and work things out with your bedroom door closed if you want to, and then let your child see you and your spouse share a kiss or at least engage in a little good-humored banter.

   Such resolution, say family researchers E. Mark Cummings and Patrick Davies in their book *Children and Marital Conflict,* "appears to act as a 'wonder drug' on children's perceptions of adults' fights, putting the conflict in a relatively positive rather than highly negative light in their eyes."

- *Be reassuring and honest to your child.* Say to him, "Mom and I did have a fight, but this is something we'll work out and I want you to know you're not to blame." Don't deny that anything unpleasant happened.

GOOD GUY/BAD GUY: PARENT-PARENT SABOTAGE

Parents who regularly are at loggerheads won't have much difficulty spotting these tendencies in themselves and then, ideally, taking some steps to strengthen the healthy adult/child alignments of the family triangle.

There's another kind of parental behavior that, if consistently engaged in or carried to the far end of the continuum, can derail the maintenance of positive triangulation: one parent fosters a parent/child versus parent alignment, a teaming up that may seem quite harmless and is often hard to identify.

In many households, Mom and Dad naturally and mostly unconsciously alternate between being "good guy" and "bad guy." Perhaps Mom is usually the homework police, while Dad takes a more laid-back, "let the kid relax awhile first" position. But Dad may be the stickler about bedtime, while Mom doesn't mind their child staying up for one more round of stories or one more cartoon video.

"I'm the one with the open-purse attitude," says the mother of a teenage son, "so I'm the one Tim always comes to for money. He'll say, 'I need some cash—okay, Mom?' and I'll say, 'Sure. Take what you need out of my bag.' I don't think he abuses this, and I know he really does have some purpose or need when he asks. But Ed tells me I'm not doing our son any favor by being such a soft touch. So then sometimes I close up the purse strings for a while and say we have to stick to the allowance we've worked out."

All children—and especially only children, because they are so intensely tuned in to mother/father/child dynamics—learn which parent is "good" for what. In normally harmonious families—with parents who have a healthy regard for their differences, a useful degree of self-awareness, and an underlying commitment to the parenting team—good guy/bad guy divisions even out over the long haul. Sometimes Mom is the heavy, some-times she's the softie, and sometimes Dad plays those roles. Splits and preferences and what's coming from Mommy and what from Daddy balance themselves out; the pendulum keeps a steady rhythm.

The danger comes when one parent repeatedly and subtly lines up the child on his or her side. Even in a solid marriage between loving parents, this kind of teaming up—which amounts to subliminal sabotage of one grown-up by the other—can take place.

Parents of only children, of course, receive all their parenting satisfactions from just one child; their sense of themselves as suc-cessful or loved or "good" parents comes from that single source. And sometimes a parent may, unconsciously, have a deep-seated need to feel like her child's favorite, to be perceived by him as the benevolent one or the concerned one.

"I'll help you with your project—your father is busy reading," says Mom. Or Mom returns a gift that the child received because it wasn't assembled just right, and Dad says, "Your mother's such a perfectionist, isn't she? Nothing is ever quite good enough for her." Or Dad, with a wink at his daughter, slips the child some cookies that Mom has said no to.

We all do a little of this, without any great harm being per-petrated. But if that sort of interaction happens a lot, there's a subtle message conveyed: I'm more available than he is, or, I'm easier-going and more flexible, or, I'm more generous than she is. That may in fact be true, but there's a low-key kind of under-mining going on at the same time. When one parent regularly projects a vaguely negative or critical attitude about the other, she sets up a situation in which her child may begin to perceive his parents as pitted against each other. And then every child's desire to get what he wants when he wants it will mean he may feel free to go about trying to divide and conquer the parenting team.

SUBLIMINAL PARENT-PARENT SABOTAGE: HOW TO SPOT IT, HOW TO STOP IT

Do you hear yourself or your spouse regularly make remarks to your child about his other parent that, in words or tone, sound like put-downs? Or maybe you know that you or your spouse regularly grants privileges to your child that the other objects to or has forbidden. Those are ways in which one of you might, unconsciously, be trying to curry favor with your child and win a little parental popularity contest.

Have you become aware that your youngster routinely approaches one and not the other of you when he wants a particular item, permission, or favor? Or have you noticed that you and your spouse often get fed separate stories by your child about what the other parent had to say concerning some item, permission, or favor? ("Mom doesn't mind if I set up the train set now. Will you help me?" said an eight-year-old to his father. Dad didn't want to get out the trains because the family soon had to leave for a visit to the in-laws, but—not wanting to be the no-sayer and the bad guy—he agreed. Mom also didn't want the trains out right then, and what she had actually said to her son a minute earlier, when he asked when he could play with his trains, was "Soon.")

Those may be signs that your child is getting good at manipulating you both to take advantage of a parent's desire to play the favorite.

If you are conscious of any of these signs, signals, or scenarios in your household, it's time to shore up the parent/parent side of the triangle. Here's how you might do so:

- *If you hear yourself* making mildly deflating remarks about your spouse in front of your child, be aware that you may be trying to plump yourself up a little in your child's eyes at your spouse's expense—and break the habit.

(One mother tells this story on herself: "My husband is a superefficient housekeeper, the one who's always wrapping the leftovers in plastic wrap, wiping off the bathroom sink with paper towels, rinsing out the trash pail with disinfectant. I, on the other hand, am exceedingly more casual about housework—and no doubt guilt-ridden because of that! One day I heard five-year-old Janice say to her father, 'Oh, Daddy, you're such a Mr. Clean!' in a kind of sarcastic or pitying tone. And I realized she got that from me. I'm always calling him Mr. Clean or Mr. Happy Housekeeper or Mr. Tidy, in front of her. Maybe because I don't want her to know her father is better at this stuff than I am.")

- *If you feel your spouse is guilty* of making put-down remarks about you, consider that he's probably unaware of what he's doing and mention it to him in private.

- *If your child seems to be perfecting* his divide-and-conquer tactics, regularly "working" one of you against the other, do some repair of the parental united front. When your child is agitating for some privilege or permission, say, "Let's go inside and see what Dad thinks," or, "Mom and I will have to talk about that before I can say yes." And then, preferably in your child's presence, discuss with your spouse the issue at hand. When he sees that his parents are going to be comparing notes and reaching joint decisions, your child starts to learn that dividing and conquering isn't going to work.

DAMAGED TRIANGLES: WHEN THE MARRIAGE IS TROUBLED

Emotional teaming up, undermining, parent-parent sabotage, and other triadic entrapments can become particularly prevalent and damaging, of course, when a marriage is rocky. And the only child is especially vulnerable to being drawn into marital stresses and strains.

She's likely to be acutely aware of tensions between her parents, because she spends so much time with them and is so much a part of their lives. She is likely, in the egocentric manner of all children, to feel that their problems stem from their parenting role—and since she is the only child around, that means she's to blame and, perhaps, she's the one who has to fix things. And when a mother or father is unhappy in the adult relationship, it's easy for that parent to seek out the child as ally or comforter.

In such situations, that youngster may assume various inappropriate roles within the triangle.

THE CHILD AS MARRIAGE COUNSELOR

When a marriage is deteriorating or troubled, the triangle can take on the dynamics of persecutor, victim, and rescuer, with the child as the rescuer or marriage counselor.

The father of an eighteen-year-old only child remembers his daughter's behavior during some turbulent years in his now more stable and sanguine marriage: "Justine and I got married because she was pregnant—we were both divorced, no kids, getting older, and we realized we really wanted a child, so we went ahead. And we both were and are crazy about Amy, but if it weren't for her, Justine and I would never have been married or stayed married. So it hasn't been smooth sailing.

"During the early years, I was often very angry with my wife, and Amy got very protective of her. I remember sometimes Justine and I would get into an argument and Amy—just four or five at the time—would call her mother: 'Mom, come here, look, I want to show you this.' Justine would go into her room, and Amy would start talking a mile a minute and try to get her involved in some game. It was obvious that this little tiny kid was trying to take care of her mother and break up the argument."

Another couple went through a difficult and tense two years while the husband was unemployed and trying, with limited success, to set up a consulting business out of the family's apartment. "We never had fights," says the wife, "but I know I was deeply disappointed in Larry and felt he should be trying harder to get his rear in gear about business, so sometimes you could cut the tension with a knife. And Marc, who was nine and ten at the time, picked up on this and would 'help' his father. He'd try to organize Larry's work area. Once he actually went out and bought a package of manila folders for his dad to use as clipping files. It was very sweet, but it was deeply disturbing to me to realize our only child felt so burdened by what was going on."

THE CHILD AS SPOUSE

Especially with the older only child—the mid or upper teenager—it can be very tempting and seductive for an unhappy mate to vent rage toward a spouse with the child and to seek consolation from the child. If a mother and her eighteen-year-old daughter are close, for example, it may be hard for that mother to resist confiding in her child about her own problems and animosities.

Or the temptation may lie in turning the child into a surrogate spouse, using the child's company as a way of meeting emotional needs the marriage is no longer filling. One father of a sixteen-year-old only—his marriage so shaky that divorce seems inevitable—calls his daughter "my best girl." The two go out together each evening on after-dinner "coffee dates," spending an hour or so sitting and talking in an outdoor café across from their apartment building.

While a father and daughter spending such time together need not necessarily be unhealthy, it seems likely in this case that the parent is using his child to fill a void—even if he is not actively bad-mouthing her mother or seeking to get his daughter "on his side." That can be terribly burdensome to the teenager, who already senses that her parents aren't getting along and is at the point in her own life where she is building relationships with boys and learning about trust and commitment.

A mother whose marriage is filled with frictions and who harbors many angry feelings toward her spouse recognized the danger of venting her complaints to her fourteen-year-old daughter and was careful not to do so. She was surprised and concerned when, one day, "Emily said to me, 'What are the things you really can't stand about Dad?' I said something innocuous, like I wish he'd put his socks in the laundry bag. Then she went through a little litany of things—he always slams the bathroom door against the wall when he opens it, he gets up in the middle of the night to eat and makes too much noise, and so on."

This mother sensed, she says, "that my daughter was promoting a 'dump Dad' conversation. I felt that she was encouraging me, in a sense, to talk to her about all the gripes I had about her father that I really should have been talking to *him* about." She resolved to make a greater effort to improve the communication between herself and her husband.

THE CHILD AS DIVORCE ATTORNEY

A woman now in her mid-twenties, an only child, still vividly remembers spending much of her youth as the go-between for her battling parents, who eventually separated. When her parents were not speaking to each other, which was often, Karen was literally the message carrier: "Go tell your father . . . ," her mother would say; "Tell your mother . . . ," said her father.

Especially when parents are in the process of divorcing or have divorced, it can be acutely difficult for them to avoid talking to each other *through* their child. Divorce is always nasty, painful, and sad. The couples I see who are going through that difficult time are usually full of rage for each other, very far away from civilized and constructive talk.

One recently separated couple, each parent deeply devoted to their nine-year-old daughter, relied on the child to convey to each other all the details concerning each week's visitation plans—when Dad was coming to pick her up, what clothing or other items she needed to bring, when she'd be returned, and so on. The girl often became tense and a little frantic that she would not remember everything correctly. Her parents were so consumed by their own anger and upset toward each other that they inappropriately used their child as a go-between. (We'll talk more in a later chapter about the special concerns of the divorced parents of an only child.)

Whenever a marriage is going through a bad patch or seriously deteriorating, the primary goal of the adults in the threesome must be to help their child feel as safe, secure, and untroubled as possible. That means:

- *Strive to keep the family emotionally whole.* It's especially critical in only-child families that parents respect and support each other *as parents,* because the only child is more likely than her siblinged peers to tend toward intense idealizations of both Mom and Dad. You owe it to your child to ensure that she is able to maintain a loving connection with each of her parents. That means you must try very hard not to attack or denigrate each other to or in front of your youngster.

- *Never let a child turn into rescuer,* counselor, confidant, or intermediary. That constitutes, for the child, a scary and damaging reversal of roles, in which the one who is smaller, younger, and more defenseless must become the bulwark of the threesome.

- *Although it is up to the adults* to try to solve their marital problems without involving the child, it can be damaging to pretend to a youngster that nothing unpleasant is going on—when it's painfully obvious to everyone, including her, that something is.

Parents have a hard time, understandably, telling a child about an impending separation or divorce. Indeed, says Judith Wallerstein, founder of the Center for the Family in Transition and coauthor of *Second Chances,* a book about families and divorce: "Despite the tremendous proliferation of media attention to divorce, nearly 50 percent of the families that we counsel waited until the day of the separation or afterward to tell their children that their familiar world is coming apart." If the marriage is beyond repair, then it can actually be a relief to a child for a parent to acknowledge the difficulty and, at the same time, reassure the youngster that both his parents love him and will do everything they can to keep him safe and happy.

During all the years your only child is growing into young adulthood, the currents that flow in the parent/parent/child triangle will be shifting and changing. The conformations will be formed by what your child needs at different stages in his development, and by how you and your spouse respond to those needs and to each other, not only as parents but as partners.

I hope you will remember what I am persuaded is the main ingredient to healthy triangulation in the three-member family: Parents need to perceive themselves as and act as the grown-ups and need to let their child remain the child.

· 8 ·

Keeping the Pressure Off

How to Avoid "Superchild Syndrome"

In my practice, I have met wonderful, caring, terribly eager and earnest parents who are determined to do right by their only child.

Many of them are accomplished professionals who have enjoyed great success in their careers or fields of interest through their own intelligence, drive, discipline, and energy. Most of these modern-day parents are well-informed, too, with more knowledge and awareness than their own parents had of the psychological "inner workings" of growing children. They read child-raising articles, they attend lectures and parenting workshops. They are able and eager to expend time and sometimes considerable resources in giving their one child what they intend to be a perfect start in life.

Given all this wind in their sails, many of these parents fully expect to enjoy the same measure of "success" as parents that they have experienced in their private or professional lives. They plan to raise a child they can view with pride as well as love—with satisfaction in their own "job well done."

All this is good. All this, also, can run the risk of turning into too much of a good thing. Those hopeful and loving efforts to have a child turn out wonderfully well have real benefits. We know that many only children are high achievers and confident people, and that that has much to do with being the sole recipients of parents' attentions.

Trouble looms, however, when a parent, with perhaps the best intentions, consistently pressures a child to become what he cannot be or does not want to be, to become a "superchild" who shines in all areas.

The only child is the repository for all his parents' expectations about being a parent. Determined to do the best by him, they also want the best from him. They want him to be an achiever *and* to enjoy a problem-free youth. If that seems not to be coming true, they may feel it is up to them to try harder, to push more, to *make happen* what they want to happen. They may be caught up in "superchild syndrome," losing sight of where their own perceptions of themselves as "successful" parents and their own wishes for their child may interfere with their youngster's healthy, necessary efforts toward separation and growth.

Mention "pressuring a child" and, I think, most readers will conjure up an image of the driven parent who from day one is going to *see to it* that his child goes to the best schools, becomes the star scholar and star athlete, goes into the best (most prestigious *and* most lucrative) career, and so on. And you might be saying, "That's not me. I would never do that kind of pushing and prodding."

But in smaller, subtler ways, parents can pressure their youngster and cause the whole family to feel the stress of superchild syndrome. Avoiding the syndrome sometimes calls for a parent to temper her own frustrations, anxieties, or worries. In this chapter and the next, we'll explore ways to do that.

SUPERCHILD SYNDROME: THE PARAMETERS

Before we talk more about how to spot signs of superchild syndrome going on in your own household—and how to get out of it—two observations will help bring into perspective what it is and what it is not.

First, of course you want the best for your child, and that may include being better or other than you were. From the moment they learn she's pregnant, a man and woman feel an aspiration to improve on their own lives in their child. That may happen in the smallest ways—for example, a baby smiles a lot, and her parents, both of whom tend to get depressed, are elated: "Look! She's smiling. She's not depressed."

So, too, do the values you hold as an individual and as a family come to bear on what you hope for and expect from your child. All this means that you will naturally project an agenda of your own onto that youngster.

Second, an agenda *should* be projected. Part of your job as a parent is to guide your child, and guiding involves some pushing. That's good for the child. Guiding, and sometimes pushing, lets your child know that you're invested in her, that you're setting a tone of what her family is all about and to which she can respond.

It's clear, I think, that we're talking about a continuum—parental feelings and behaviors that are necessary, healthy, and positive but that, if carried to an extreme, can cause trouble.

When your investment in having your child be something—be a star pupil who gets all A's, be a doctor just like you are or a violinist just like you wanted to be, be feisty or popular or athletic—is very powerful, then you almost inevitably will lose the flexibility you need to let your child lead the way. You will be tempted again and again to control matters so that your child goes down a certain pathway, and your child will suffer if that turns out not to be his own pathway.

Letting your child lead is really the best way I can summarize what is involved in avoiding the superchild syndrome. And letting your child lead while you are still guiding and encouraging him involves appreciating the fine distinction between promoting and pressuring.

Before we talk about how to promote, not pressure, see if you spot any of the following tendencies in yourself or your spouse.

ARE YOU CAUGHT UP IN THE SYNDROME?

- *Your child says,* "Look at this painting I made." You say, "Mmm, very nice . . . what about that math homework?" because at some level it bothers you that your child may show talents and preferences for artistic endeavors while you want him to go into science or business someday.

    This is an exaggeration, of course. Most parents do applaud their child's accomplishments, whatever they may be. (And in this small imaginary scenario, there might be a parent's very real practical concerns about whether her child will be adequately prepared for the job world.) But do you routinely tend to show less interest in or support for enthusiasms or skills your child reveals that you put little store in?

- *You feel at some level* that your child will not reach his best potential unless you see to it that he does. You believe that whether he achieves or not has mostly to do with your own efforts.

- *You can't let it go* if an activity you want your child to pursue is not working or is against his wishes. Backing off is difficult or even intolerable.

- *You become aware*—from feelings of anxiety or an inability to put what's going on with your child out of your mind—that a lot, a *whole* lot, of your emotional life is riding on what your child is doing or not doing at any particular time. Perhaps you sense that something is awry in the balance between the enjoyment you take in your child and the concerns you have for him. There is more worry than enjoyment, and when you can step aside and view things objectively, you *know* that your worries are exaggerated.

- *You become aware* that your child is showing signs of being under pressure.

Children can reveal in many ways that they are feeling overly pushed or pressured.

A child may very specifically and actively be protesting something you have lined up for him. Or he may *un*specifically but actively be showing that he's unhappy toward a parent by being totally uncooperative and generally a pain in the neck. Frequently in my practice, I see a child who displays feelings of intense anger about his home life, yet he would be unable to say just what's bothering him because he doesn't know. His gripe against his parent may manifest itself as: "Nothing Mom does is right." There is an overall feeling that something is wrong.

On the other hand, and very commonly, a child may be too eager to please, too compliant, yet clearly uncomfortable—nervous, fretful, not terribly happy. An only child, in particular, may tend to override her own anger and aggression at being pressured, and smooth things over by "being good." She senses that it really is her job to be the child her parents want.

She will try to be accommodating because she does not want to disappoint her parent. In addition, she may feel her parents' wishes or agenda have more validity than her own—if Mother and Father want this, it must be the thing to do. A wish, activity, or goal may not seem to have the right backing or substance, may not "ring true," unless it comes from her parents.

The only child under pressure isn't going to be able to fight back as well, to counter those forces as easily, as the youngster with siblings probably will. Remember that with a sibling in the house, a child has more pathways for discharging aggression. To say "Get away from me!" or "Leave me alone!" to a parent is scary. How much easier it is to deal with those feelings by picking a fight with a brother or sister.

The mother of a preteen says about her husband, James: "*His* son is going to Harvard, no question about it! *His* son is going to be athletic and popular and make a million bucks someday. The fact is that Jimmy is a delightful kid but not a spectacular student and not a czar of Wall Street in the making."

Jimmy's mother is "absolutely sure," she says, "that if we had more than just the one child, that lasar beam from James would be diffused. In my own family, with four of us, my sisters and brother and I all had different roles we were going to play out, according to my parents. That had its good and its bad aspects, of course, but at least no one of us felt all that pressure to be everything, the way I think Jimmy does."

Her husband's constant "boring in" on their son, says Jimmy's mother, and his often unrealistic expectations have, she feels, been hard on Jimmy. "I think he's an anxious kid, very eager to please his father, very hard on himself when he thinks he's not measuring up. He doesn't seem to get a whole lot of fun out of life! And James and I are always arguing about this, from Jimmy's homework to what friends he has to whether he should sign up for a super computer course after school."

When one parent is intensely invested in all the child's successes or disappointments, while the other parent has a more "let the kid live his own life" attitude, special tensions exist that may permeate all the small and large issues involved in child raising. Later, we'll talk about some ways a parent who feels a spouse is excessively pressuring their child might improve the situation.

For now, just remember that a child who, like Jimmy, seems regularly anxious, overly striving, or disappointed in himself, or a child who vociferously protests an agenda that has been laid out before him, or a child who seems often mad at the world for reasons that are not clear, may be feeling the effects of superchild syndrome.

In these ways, he may be letting his parents know that they have crossed the line from promoting to pressuring.

Here are some ideas to think about and suggestions to implement that will help you keep the pressure off:

KNOW WHEN TO INSIST ON EXTRAS, WHEN TO SUGGEST THEM, AND WHEN TO DROP IT

Many parents of only children line up lots of extracurricular activities for their youngsters, in efforts to involve them with other children, broaden their experiences, and help them to develop a variety of skills or areas of learning. Some children enjoy this kind of busyness, others might prefer less of it.

It is quite appropriate to insist that your child pursue an area, such as religious education, that has deep meaning to you and your values as a family. Your child may not routinely *love* having to attend religious classes. He may never even give you the satisfaction of saying, five or ten years down the road, that he's glad you made him go. He may look back and still feel resentful at having been forced to do something every Saturday morning when he really wanted to be out with his friends! But you are saying, in effect: I am the parent, and I need to guide you in a way that I feel is important.

Many children also routinely don't love taking the piano lessons or the swimming lessons or participating in other learning experiences that their parents think are good for them, and in these areas it's probably wise to attempt to walk a fine line between suggesting *and* pushing. Certainly it's a mistake to propel a youngster over a long period of time along a route for which he has no particular aptitude or enthusiasm. But so many of us adults do look back and say, "I'm so glad my mother made me take those piano lessons, even though I didn't want to do it at the time and hated practicing and I can't play very well now."

Your child can benefit from sampling a variety of activities, and I think it's all to the good to suggest that he try one or more. It is wonderfully enriching when one of them "takes" and he goes on to develop a serious enthusiasm or master a skill that gives him pride and pleasure.

Even when something doesn't take, and even when the idea is mostly yours and not his, in the long run it may not have been a mistake.

One mother took her young daughter to ice-skating lessons every weekend for three years, "because I wanted her to appreciate that she had a good, well-coordinated, athletic body," she says, "and more than that, to get an idea of what it's like to master a skill, to appreciate little measures of improvement that came from her sticking to it. But I dragged her there every Saturday." Now, many years later, this teenager loves showing an occasional friend the videotape of her performance in a skating sequence. "I think she's pleased that she could do that," says her mother, "and in retrospect, it seems like it wasn't a bad idea to make her go. While it was going on, sometimes I thought: This is crazy—*I* want her to skate, *she* doesn't."

Over the course of your child's development, there may be many such happenings. If you trust your own judgment, if you pay attention to the signals from your child, doing a little such pushing will probably be, as this mother says, not a bad idea.

But if your child is really bucking doing something you want her to do, really unhappy, if her objections are more than the ordinary "I don't feel like going because it's hard to do and I'd rather watch cartoons" protests, then it is probably wise to drop it. Question whether you have an agenda of your own that is really too much or too wrong for your child. If the idea of dropping lessons that aren't working or that your child hates is very upsetting to you, the chances are that you are pushing a superchild syndrome.

KNOW YOUR OWN "SOFT SPOTS"—AREAS OF CRAZINESS AND ANXIETY TRIGGERS

As we have said before, it's natural for parents to want their child to have it better than they had it, to not make the same mistakes or suffer the same kind of growing pains they may still remember with discomfort. That can lead a mother or father to become overly focused on one particular aspect of their child's personality or behavior and then become overly invested in "correcting" what they see as a problem.

A father who regrets his inability to take part in sports in his youth might pressure his equally unathletic son to join teams. A parent whose own school years were marked by academic struggles may become upset or enraged if her child brings home a C or two.

For one mother, her excruciating shyness as a child assumed in her mind the proportions almost of a disease, one that she constantly worried her daughter would inherit. In an effort to prevent that from happening, she made considered and appropriate efforts to give her only child the kind of support in developing friendships that she felt she had never received from her own mother: She invited other children regularly to their home and in other ways tried to help her rather quiet child feel comfortable with her peers.

But when a play date didn't seem to be going well, when her daughter wasn't invited to anybody else's home over a week or two, this mother became, she says, "beside myself with worry and anxiety. It's amazing I didn't give myself an ulcer." She feels now that she was "going at" her child all the time, urging her to call friends, to make new friends, to "act nicer."

Identifying your own soft spots, the aspects of your life that you'd hate to see your child repeat, can help you recognize when you may be crossing the line into overinvestment and pressuring. Your child may indeed be having a little problem, wrestling through a little passage of growing up; all children, being human, will have their internal foes to face from time to time. But your own feelings of anxiety, of being on the verge of an ulcer, will make matters worse. Your child then may realize that you're looking at her and seeing something wrong. The very best you can do as a parent is to be available, be supportive, and try to be objective.

MODERATE YOUR PRAISE

An eight-year-old girl had been painstakingly working on a card for her grandfather, complete with "balloon" letters, each painted in with a different color. Her mother passed by the table where her daughter was drawing, and raved: "Oh, baby, that's *gorgeous!* He is going to *love* it!" The little girl stopped her coloring, looked at her artwork, and said, "No, it's not at all gorgeous." She crumpled up the paper and threw it away.

Her mother, later, talked about her child's tendency to be what she called "a violent perfectionist. I always try to praise her a lot, so she won't be so hard on herself."

That mother's intentions were good, and perhaps her daughter can be gently helped not to be so hard on herself. But consistent, excessive praise may backfire. I suspect that youngster had an image in her mind of how her artwork should look, found the reality not measuring up to the image, and didn't want to hear that it was "gorgeous" when she believed it was just okay. Very possibly, too, she had concluded over time that her mother's reactions to her efforts didn't meet a reality test. Once they grow beyond the very early stage of feeling they are invincible, children acquire a keen sense of how they compare with other children in various ways.

Parents of an only child, I have found, tend to "inflate" their child, because for one thing, they do see her as the single most wonderful creature in the universe. For another, many of today's self-aware, psychologically sensitive mothers and fathers have come to conclude that their own self-esteem was diminished as a child, and they hope to imbue their youngster with a stronger sense of self. And so they are constantly pumping the child up with lots of praise, exploding with delight over some accomplishment for which a sincere "Good for you" would be more fitting.

Again in my experience, that's a tendency especially evident with a parent or parents who are out of the home, working at jobs. The employed mother is not around all day to say, "Oh, that was nice what you did with your dolly," and then, a bit later, "I can't come and look at your castle right now—maybe in a minute or two." There is a different rhythm to the day when the mother is home, one in which little episodes fit in and harmonize with each other—small moments of praise or small reprimands, balancing each other out in a bigger context.

If you're an employed mother, chances are that as you rejoin your child at the end of the day you feel a need to be supernice, superinterested in everything she does. You feel you must build her up, and so you may react with excessively "up" emotions.

That can constitute a kind of pressure for your child. Temper those inclinations:

- *Praise your child* when and where praise is due. But listen to yourself over a period of time, and see if you're overdoing it. Your child will surely pick up any false notes.

- *Acknowledge small achievements* with small compliments or words of appreciation. It's awfully nice—and it builds self-esteem—for your child to hear Mom or Dad say, "I really liked the way you shared your blocks with your cousin today," or, "You got an eighty-three on your math test? The last one was a seventy-five. You're doing better. Good work." The mother of that girl who became so abruptly unhappy with her drawing might have kept the pressure off by remarking casually that she liked the way the "B" was turning out or that the combination of colors was very pretty.

ACKNOWLEDGE YOUR OWN DOWN TIMES

For many employed parents, "down" times are most intense when they come home at the end of a long workday and then reenter their parenting roles. That 6-to-8 P.M. transition can be very trying. You may desperately need a little of your "own" time but consider it not fair to your child if you take it. You may feel especially guilty because there is only one child at home. But your youngster can get an inflated sense of her own place if she's never impelled to recognize that her parents have needs separate from her own. Trying always to be a superparent feeds into the superchild syndrome.

One father contrasts the after-work scene he remembers from his childhood with what happens in his own home. "My dad got home around six, and his routine was always the same. My brother, sister, and I were usually doing homework or stuff, waiting for dinner. Dad gave us all a quick 'Hi, how was school today?' and then went upstairs to wash up and change out of his suit and tie. Then he came back down, poured himself a drink, and sat reading the paper until dinner.

"When I get home from work," continues this father of a four-year-old, "I open the door, and Polly shrieks 'Daddy!' and jumps into my arms. That is probably the greatest moment in my entire day. Then I'm supposed to be her horsie or whatever else she's got in mind. Then I start thinking it would be nice to have a little time to shift gears on my own! I get a second wind later in the evening, and Polly and I always do things together after her bath. But as much as I hate to admit it, I wouldn't mind having a little time without her to unwind, like my dad."

Another parent tells almost the same story. "I think if I had two or three kids," says the mother of a five-year-old who is cared for during the afternoon by a baby-sitter, "I'd probably be able to come home, give each one a kiss, and say, 'Now you all go watch cartoons while I get some dinner going.' With Pam, I get home and she's all over me. Lately, she wants to play store, and she has this game all set up and ready to go the minute I'm home. And I do adore seeing her again and I like playing with her, but I also would like to read the mail and take my shoes off and chill out a little! Yet I don't want her to think that she doesn't come first."

Feeling guilty about feeling stressed out at the end of the day is not pleasant. Take some of the pressure off yourself:

- *Recognize that you're tired or conflicted,* that maybe you aren't really up to meeting your child's demands—and that it's normal. Just acknowledging those emotions to yourself can put you in a much better state than if you fiercely deny feelings you think are "wrong" and are determined to be sweet, pleasant, and fully present in body, mind, and spirit.

- *If you are not desperate* to have a little time out for yourself when you first arrive home but are thinking of all the things you need to get done, try taking the first fifteen or twenty minutes to focus completely on your child. Put out of your mind starting dinner or reading mail, and tell yourself, "For right now, I am going to forget about everything else and give myself over to enjoying these minutes with my child."

  If your child is in a standoffish mood—and many youngsters do need to "warm up" again to the parents they haven't seen all day—take that time to just sit together or maybe quietly join him in his play. You will relieve your own pressures if you consciously decide to spend some minutes doing nothing but reconnecting with your child in a relaxed way.

- *If you do want or need* to do other things, tell your child: "I really want to hear what you have to tell me/play that game with you, so let's do it after dinner, when I won't be so rushed and I can pay attention better. And if I forget, you come and remind me." Even a very young child can temper his desire for your attentions if he understands that later you'll be "all there" for him.

WORK WITH YOUR SPOUSE TO PROMOTE, NOT PRESSURE

It often happens that one parent is intensely invested in his only child and makes her the repository of all his own hopes, expectations, and agendas, while his spouse is keenly aware that their child is having a hard time fulfilling those hopes and is suffering because of it.

If you feel that your partner is excessively enmeshed in your child's successes or failures, is consistently and unrealistically pressuring him to achieve, is unaware of signs of strain or distress you recognize in your youngster:

- *Try to convey your feelings* to your spouse in a constructive dialogue. This takes some determination and some planning; it's not easy and there's no guarantee talking will solve the problem, but as the grown-ups of your family threesome, it behooves you both to give it a try.

  Pick a time and place when you and your spouse will be able to talk calmly (not during or just after an argument) and in the absence of your child. Start things off by acknowledging your common ground: "You love our daughter, I love our daughter, we both want what's best for her. It's not to her benefit if we're sending her double messages about our expectations."

  State what's bothering you, in specific, nonaccusatory terms: "I think Jenny feels overloaded because she's trying to do too much too perfectly right now, and that's why she's having trouble settling down to sleep at night." Not: "You expect too much from Jenny and you're turning her into a basket case."

Come up with one or two realistic small steps you can implement right away: "I think she'd really like it if you spent some relaxed time with her in the evening. She's especially into drawing these days. Maybe you can draw pictures together for twenty minutes or so."

• *Network with other parents.* Try to increase the time you spend with other mothers and fathers and talk about child problems and situations. Your spouse might be open to fresh ideas and insights when they come from outside your own tight family circle.

DON'T FEEL OBLIGED TO BE PERPETUALLY ENTERTAINING

Says the father of a preteen: "On weekends and on the long summer vacations I get as a teacher, I used to go to great lengths to make sure we had something neat lined up to do all the time. Even today, Carrie will still come to me and say, 'What are we going to do now?'"

Another parent, the divorced mother of a fourteen-year-old, echoes that thought. "Why do we all think we have to entertain our kids? When she was little, I used to play games with Elizabeth all evening until her bedtime. And then it was a struggle getting her down! My time came after she went to sleep. My sister did the same thing, and at bedtime she was ordered to sit on the landing outside her kid's room so Penny could see her until she fell asleep. And my sister did this night after night."

Interestingly, both that father and that mother talk about very different experiences from their own childhoods. Carrie's father remembers summer afternoons "when I'd climb up on the roof of this little bungalow we rented at the shore and just lie there very contentedly for hours. Nobody fussed with me or worried about what I was doing."

Elizabeth's mother says she would frequently "trot around with my mother while she did her stuff, like going to the supermarket or whatever. I remember flipping through magazines in the beauty parlor while she got a perm, which seemed to take hours. In the afternoons after school, she'd be doing housework and dinner, and I was expected to amuse and occupy myself."

That urge to be perpetually entertaining companions to our children—which inevitably is most intense in the only-child home—stems, I think, from several sources. Previous generations seemed to maintain a more "children are children and grown-ups are grown-ups" attitude, and parents saw their child-raising roles primarily as provider, educator, and moral conscience. In addition, today's employed parents want the relatively limited time they have with their child to be as pleasurable as they can make it. And of course, the parents of an only who has nothing to do tend to think that child is lonely or unhappy, and that it's up to them to fix it.

Reduce that pressure on yourself:

- *Don't feel you must be* your child's perpetual playmate. Leave her often to her own resources, and you help her grow and find her own pathways in life.

- *Don't feel everything you do* together must be "fun." Although your child may protest at having to "tag along" while Mom gets her hair done or Dad has the oil in the car changed—and although he may complain loudly about being bored—there can be something very secure and deeply comforting for a child in experiencing in these routine ways that he is the child and you are the grown-up, and that children and grownups do different things.

RESPECT YOUR CHILD'S INTERESTS

I hear many parents of only children fret about the fact that their youngster "isn't interested in anything." And very often, what they actually mean is that the child has shown no inclination for what they themselves consider worthwhile pursuits.

The father of a nine-year-old boy was upset, even angry, about the fact that, he said, "the only thing this kid gets stirred up about is his miniature car collection. Forget about reading books. Forget about learning."

The mother of a fifteen-year-old girl was frantic because her daughter's whole world revolved around her social life. "All that matters to her are her friends," said this mother. "She's naturally a very talented artist, but she does nothing with it at all. I've tried to get her to take studio classes, start getting a portfolio worked up that she'll have ready to show in a few years for art school or whatever. But she ignores me."

Both of these children were doing adequately in school. Both were contented youngsters who were getting on with life. And what is important in this context, both had an interest from which they were drawing pleasure.

Psychologists know that a child who is able to make an investment in something other than his parents is probably basically in good shape. That ability to focus away from the mother and father toward an interest that has some mileage, that provides another avenue for involvement and satisfaction, is an indication of real growth capacity. Over time, it will evolve, undergo many shapes and changes as a youngster moves toward adulthood, but the important core quality is that the child is able to engage with something—and playing with miniature cars and having many friends are valid demonstrations of that kind of engagement.

Overall, you will use your good judgment as a way of monitoring what's going on. Of course, if your child is focused in one arena to the complete exclusion of all other areas of life, there's nothing wrong with offering some suggestions, doing a little pushing. If she's totally "into" her social life with friends, by all means say, Maybe you want to read a book. It is part of your role as a parent to try to bring balance into your child's life.

But don't cross the line into forcing and pressuring toward an outlet you consider "better." If your child is interested in something or doing something that does not follow your own aspirations for her, as long as it's basically healthy and not dangerous, don't be disappointed, don't badger her to move on, and don't belittle the objects of her enthusiasm. If she's all caught up in making elaborate scrapbooks about movie stars, let her be—even if you consider this a superficial and frivolous waste of time. If he's a rock music fanatic, let him be—even if you'd like it a whole lot more if he'd listen to Chopin. Something is percolating with your child, and that's what counts.

KNOW THAT MANY "UNDERACHIEVERS" SOAR WHEN THEY REACH COLLEGE AGE OR YOUNG ADULTHOOD

Many parents of only children have a primary focus on their child's academic achievement and may be bitterly disappointed if their youngster regularly comes up with B's or C's in his classes. It is vital to remember that some children are not, and never will be, A students, and pressuring them in the academic arena can cause them to grow up feeling inadequate despite other things that they may do positively and well.

Some children, too, don't hit their stride until the childhood years are over. The father of a son who now, in his mid-twenties, is forging a satisfying and exciting career traveling all over the world as a petroleum engineer, says he often despaired that his young boy "would never grow up and leave home.

"He loved all sports, but he was an indifferent student," says this father. "He still liked to watch early-morning cartoons on TV when he was fourteen. Sometimes it seemed to me that he was in a perpetual fog. Then, two years into college, pow—everything seemed to come together for him."

Remember that early academic success is not necessarily an accurate predictor of success in life. Psychologists really know very little still about why people achieve, nor can they define or understand in an absolute way what achievement is.

REMIND YOURSELF THAT MANY FACTORS ARE INFLUENCING YOUR CHILD

One of the elements of the superchild syndrome lies in a parent's conviction that she has the power to shape her youngster along a particular pathway. As a parent, you can guide, suggest, promote, and even push, but in the final analysis, a child's road is his own. It develops out of his unique structure and personality. It develops, too, from what goes on in the complex world outside the family.

It is always difficult for a parent fully to appreciate the separateness of her child. It's a good idea to tell yourself occasionally that chances are your child is not going to be what you want him to be. And that's all right. Through my work with children, I have come to have great admiration for the generation in which your only child is starting out his life. So many young people I see have remarkable values and strengths—for sustaining friendships, for appreciating qualities of character, for moving toward their own achievements.

Your job is to provide the climate, the security, and the breathing room for your child to grow, in whatever way that is going to be.

· 9 ·
Roots and Wings

More Ideas on How to Give
Your Child Security and Freedom,
While Keeping the Pressure Off

Every loving parent instinctively knows that a child needs
roots, a secure home base that helps her feel protected,
encouraged, and confident. And then she needs wings, the experiences, courage, and sense of freedom that enable her to move
into the bigger world outside.

And every parent has to strike a fine balance between holding
on and letting go. For the parent of an only child, finding that
balance may be especially challenging.

The mother of eleven-year-old Claudia says that she and her
husband and their only child "can feel like a little universe unto
ourselves sometimes. We have great times together." The closeness and intensity of that relationship, she feels, makes it difficult
to "let go" of her child.

"I'm engaged in a little push-pull battle with myself all the
time! I want to push her out of the nest, so she'll do things, take
chances, be with other people. And then at the same time, basically I think I never want to let her out of my sight."

Claudia's mother talked to her own mother about letting children go. "She had four of us, the oldest and youngest being twelve
years apart. My mother says that there were kids around the house
for so long, by the time my little brother went off for college the
silence felt wonderful. I myself really try not to think a whole lot
about the day Claudia will leave."

Our suggestions in this chapter will, I hope, provide some added perspective on your own "letting go" processes with your only child.

SET UP LOTS OF OPPORTUNITIES FOR YOUR CHILD TO BE WITH OTHER CHILDREN

As a number of parents have indicated in the conversations that formed the basis for this book, many only children seem to have a special capacity to be content in their own company and in their parents'. Enjoying solitary pursuits or being with Mom and Dad is all to the good, as long as a youngster also has plenty of opportunities, from a young age, to be around other children and thus experience the joys and hurts of finding his place among his peers.

Most parents tend to be acutely aware of this need to encourage child-oriented time, and they go to great lengths to make it happen, as this divorced mother of a seven-year-old reveals:

"Something about Elena is very mature, very self-sufficient. She doesn't care a great deal about socializing. She'll play by herself for hours.

"And then she wants my one-hundred-percent attention! I sometimes am concerned that I may fill too many needs, and that's not so good for either of us," Elena's mother continues. "She and I are both one-on-one people. I've always had some trouble in threesomes, and so does Elena—she fixes on one friend, and that's it. So I have always been very conscious of making play dates and seeing that she's with a variety of other kids. I am almost obsessed about it! Since she's with her father every other weekend, I'm often making Saturday play arrangements two or three weeks in advance."

More than any other factor, exposure to her peers—the play dates and the play groups and the preschool sessions—will help your young child begin to see herself as a normal child, one of many in the world. Elena's mother is wise to keep encouraging her solitary-tending daughter to spend some of her time with friends, although right now it's clearly not easy for that mother to persevere in her efforts. By the time they reach the mid–elementary school years, most children are able to start forming their own alliances and friendships, and it becomes less necessary for a parent to be social director.

And then Elena's mother—and any parent of an only child—would be especially wise to remember the next bit of advice.

SET UP THE OPPORTUNITIES . . . BUT DON'T FORCE FRIENDSHIPS

Like that mother who admitted sheepishly that when she invited children over she sometimes viewed them as "hired playmates" for her young son, it's easy for the parent of an only child to become overly invested in what's going on between the children.

One mother and father remember being frantic about finding youngsters to invite to their son's birthday party: "He was two years old! A baby. And I was worrying that he didn't have enough friends," says this father. Now that their son is thirteen, they have acquired some perspective on the matter. "Marjie and I agonized a lot about every little rejection David got over the years, about whether he was fitting in or not," says David's father. "David has made friends, and he's going to be fine. In retrospect, we would have had a lot more fun as parents if we could have been more laid back. Other kids come and go in your kid's life."

Another parent was thrilled when a couple living in the same apartment building had a baby girl just two weeks after her own daughter was born. "I envisioned these two kids being inseparable," she says, "growing up like little sisters and spending hours together in their place or ours." She befriended the other woman (who wasn't particularly responsive), joined the same mother/ baby play groups at the local Y, repeatedly invited the other youngster in for toddler play dates.

"Basically," she says, "after four or five years of forcing this thing, I admitted to myself that this kid and my kid didn't particularly like each other. And even very young children sometimes aren't going to be soul mates. The girls are now going on eleven, they're both only children, and they never have had anything much to do with each other. They don't even say hello in the elevator!"

GET THEM TOGETHER, HELP THEM ALONG . . . BUT DON'T HOVER

A very young child who is first getting used to having a youngster his own age come to his house—and play with *his* things—or first getting used to sharing sandbox space at the park will benefit from some parental play-date monitoring.

Says the mother of three-year-old Robert: "Now that Robert has started preschool, there are suddenly a lot of kids in his life. He goes to the school for two hours in the morning, and then most afternoons I'll bring some child home with us for an hour or two. It's taking him a while to adjust to this one-on-one with a kid his own age who wants the same things he wants. And also to get used to the fact that a child plays with him differently than his mom does."

Robert's mother found that her son's play dates get off to a smooth start if she stays in the same room with the two youngsters for a while and offers some suggestions on how they might play together and when it's a good time to switch toys or take turns. "Especially if the other child is kind of a rambunctious type, I play monitor," she says, "but I also try to leave them alone as much as I can."

Robert's mother, I believe, demonstrates a finely tuned sense of when it's wise to "hold on"—listening carefully and giving her son appropriate help—and when to "let go"—stepping back and letting the youngsters find their own way.

Your toddler may need you to help him figure out how to play with another child. Very young children have to be taught how to do it, and that means a parent or caregiver nearby as playtime "monitor," making sure not only that the children don't hurt each other but that they're practicing how to be appropriate social beings—sharing objects, taking turns, learning that someone else has his own ideas and wishes about what's going on. Even by ages five and six, children who are playing together still benefit from adult reminders that they need to be respectful of each other. Kindergarten children are not yet really aware that they can hurt one another by the things they say.

Paying attention and offering guidelines, however, does not mean you have to be intrusive and meddling. As the parent of an only child, you may be especially tempted to hover over your youngster's socializing, to see if she's living up to your own hopes and expectations. Says one mother: "I have definitely been guilty of micromanaging playtimes! We'd have some child over, and my antennas were up all the time. Is Carla letting herself get pushed around? Is she being too aggressive? Are they taking turns? And then I was always jumping in if I thought things weren't going right."

Your child does need to learn how to take turns, and how to stand up for herself or when to yield center stage. Those are lessons most successfully learned with gentle reminders or help from you but with a minimal amount of parental "jumping in" to solve problems.

Much research in family dynamics and in how children practice resolving conflicts shows that the more parents intervene in sibling squabbles, the more those fights occur—and the more brothers and sisters rely on Mom or Dad to solve their problems. Your child is getting those sibling rivalry experiences with friends.

ENCOURAGE RELATIONSHIPS WITH OLDER AND YOUNGER CHILDREN

"It bothers me that my son sees nothing but nine-year-old boys most of the time," says the mother of nine-year-old Patrick, who attends a single-sex school. "All the friends he sees on weekends are his classmates. I make a big effort to get other sizes in his life."

This mother believes that "knowing children of different ages gives my son a kind of barometer, something to measure his own progress by. Recently when we were visiting my sister, she happened to be measuring her kids, literally. She has three, and one thing they do is keep a height and age chart going on one wall. Her four-year-old was thrilled the day we were there because she had just gotten taller than her brother was when he was four. I was thinking of Patrick's height line on our wall back home. He doesn't get to see what he's aiming for."

All children tend to befriend and stick with youngsters their age. But the only child doesn't have the easy opportunity a child with siblings may have to observe "other sizes," brothers or sisters and their friends, in action. And it is to his benefit—part of reality testing and seeing where he fits in the greater scheme of things—for a child to "measure" himself against other youngsters in a variety of ways.

Patrick is very fond of a cousin who is two years older than he is, and Patrick's mother gets the two children together as often as possible: "I watch him with her, and there's a calmness and great pleasure in each other's company. When she slept over recently, the two of them were busy at the crack of dawn, putting out a newspaper. They're very accepting of each other, and he's very comfortable with the fact that she's older—I sense an attitude that 'she's two years older than me, so she knows more about that than I do.'"

Parents of only children tend to start stewing and worrying, I have found, if their youngster enjoys playing with younger children. They feel that this behavior is "babyish," or that their child is lagging emotionally or developmentally. Certainly there may be cause for some concern if a child repeatedly avoids youngsters his own age and appears comfortable *only* in the company of those younger than himself.

But in general, it can be both pleasurable and useful for your child to play with someone younger, perhaps helping him build blocks or work puzzles. These interactions between older and younger happen spontaneously in siblinged families, and some psychologists believe there are beneficial aspects for the older child from what they term the "mentoring factor": being able to tutor and instruct a younger child imparts a sense of competence and practice in nurturing.

SLEEPOVERS ARE A GOOD IDEA

Invite your child's friend to stay overnight or spend a weekend with your family. Let your youngster accept his friend's invitation for an overnight at his family's house. Spending extended periods of time with another child, with normal family routines going on, can help an only child enormously in that process of learning to make intimate adjustments to people other than his parents. And sleepover dates provide richly sibling-like experiences for an only child.

One mother of a nine-year-old daughter says: "When one of Corinne's friends is staying over for a night or a weekend, there's a completely different pace and atmosphere than there is if it's just a play date after school. They may stay up late if it's a Friday night, and I hear them giggling and talking in her bedroom after lights-out. Once when her best friend was over they got into a big fight, but by a couple of hours later, they were lying on her bed together, watching a video.

"The two kids will get into problems about who takes a shower first or what snacks they're going to make. Then they go on to the next thing. That kind of sister-to-sister stuff that I remember from my own childhood with my sister gets going, which I think is all to the good."

KNOW YOUR CHILD'S FRIENDS' PARENTS

"As soon as my son was born," says one mother, "I *needed* to know other new mothers. For the first couple of years, I was collecting phone numbers from anybody I'd meet in the park or the doctor's office or wherever who had a child about Christopher's age. Now he's in sixth grade, and I still try to get to know his classmates' parents. It's from other parents that I've learned the most important things I've wanted to know about raising a kid."

Parent support groups—informal get-togethers with another parent or two, or the more structured sessions that some school PTAs organize or that are offered through community facilities—can be a great way to swap child-raising stories and advice, and get a "fix" on what's typical behavior for a two- or a five- or a fifteen-year-old. We live more isolated lives than did people a generation or two ago, with parents working long job hours, with relatives scattered far afield. As the parent of an only child, you may find your closest parent-to-parent ties come about through your child's friendships and contacts. Making a parent friend is wonderful when it happens; often it doesn't.

The mother of a teenager says that when her daughter was born, a friend gave her a piece of advice that proved valuable. "My office pal had a son who was then about eleven or twelve," she says. "One day when my daughter, Becky, was a few months old, that woman and I were chatting about kids growing up, and she said, 'You're going to meet a lot of other mothers and fathers. Remember that you don't have to love them just because your kid likes their kid!'

"It's interesting to me now," Becky's mother continues, "that over the past sixteen years I've gotten to know probably dozens of other mothers, as my daughter has had various playmates and 'best friends.' Three of those women are now my closest friends. Most of the others I barely remember. I think when you have just one child you tend to get very, very caught up in the kid's social life. And I've put a lot of pressure on myself at times to try to be friends with some other child's parent."

Especially during her daughter's early school years, Becky's mother feels, she needed to have another parent like her and was at times quite distressed by a mother's unresponsiveness or the fact that a relationship remained casual and distant. "I think that having another parent like me or my liking another parent was a way of affirming myself as a good mother," she says, "and maybe a way of ensuring that our kids would continue as friends. I've had to remind myself that parents are also people, and there are a lot of people I'm never going to be on the same wavelength with."

"SHARE" YOUR CHILD WITH ONE OF YOUR CHILDLESS FRIENDS

If you're fortunate enough to have an unmarried or childless friend or friends who genuinely love being around kids, you have an opportunity to encourage a potentially rich and nourishing relationship for your youngster. This is so especially if you are a single parent or if your own extended family of grandparents, aunts, uncles, and cousins is small or too far away for regular visits.

Not all people without children, of course, are good candidates. Many parents have shared this woman's experience:

"Almost immediately after our son was born, my husband and I started seeing a whole lot less of two married, childless couples we were friends with," says the mother of Garth, who's now ten. "At first, that was just a matter of time and logistics, but it's interesting and a little sad to me that we have never really reestablished the friendships as they used to be, and we had been very close with those people. I know that both those couples elected not to have children, but they never have been especially interested in our child. We just went different ways."

But many, many adults find it most satisfying to enjoy the fun of children, while avoiding the responsibility and expense of being parents themselves.

The father of a twelve-year-old girl says that his supervisor in the city agency where he works "has adored Emma from the day she was born. Sheila hasn't married; she's about ten years older than my wife and me. And she's just clearly gotten a big kick out of playing Auntie Mame to Emma over the years. She takes her to see *The Nutcracker* ballet every winter. She has helped out at all the birthday parties. What we like seeing is that now that Emma's older, she still loves being with Sheila. It's not so much fun and games anymore, but they get into serious talks."

An article in the *New York Times* described an increasing number of what some social commentators are calling "para-parenting" arrangements, which bind children and single adults in friendships that last over many years, and which provide rich rewards for parent, friend, and child. In one such arrangement, the former roommate of the single mother of a young girl takes the child for an occasional vacation, baby-sits when possible, and is able to treat the youngster to some extras, such as piano lessons or roller skates, that the girl's mother would find difficult to afford.

What has been especially comforting to the two women is that the girl, an only child with no close relatives, clearly feels safer with her "para-parent" in her life. Her mother's friend, an unmarried professional who does not anticipate having a child of her own, provides low-key reassurance to the child that more than one grown-up is looking out for her.

Striking demographic changes in the United States in recent years underscore the fact that many grown-ups who probably do enjoy being with children are not actually living with any. Since 1970, the percentage of adults living alone has almost doubled; today, over one in four people between the ages of twenty-five and fifty-four live alone.

It's good for your youngster to have lots of grown-ups in her life. Make the effort to find friends who might become an unofficial extended family, and make them part of your life.

IF YOUR CHILD HAS A SPECIAL TALENT
OR INTEREST, ENCOURAGE IT

It's empowering and esteem-building for any child to feel he shines in one area or another. And most parents do prize and foster their children's separate enthusiasms, shepherding them to their various activities.

It can be especially good and even "useful" for an only child to develop a talent or hobby that others find entertaining or intriguing. One child, now a young man who works in the computer field, fell in love with magic when he was about ten, and developed a talent that he says "was and still is an icebreaker, and sometimes a great moneymaker too.

"I watched a guy on TV one day demonstrating some simple rope tricks, tying knots that just popped open, and I was hooked. I learned the rope tricks, then coin and card tricks. My mother and father were great about this. They got me some lessons, bought me the books and equipment. My dad slightly knew Walter Gibson, a great magician, and he arranged for me to meet him."

All through high school, he says, he earned money performing at children's parties, but the real payoff from his love of the art of magic has been "to help a shy guy like me be a hit in gatherings. People get a charge out of magic, and I love being the performer."

Pressuring a child to excel at something he really has little interest in, as we've said before, is not a good idea and won't work, and as the parent of an only, you would be wise to be conscious of any lurking intentions to turn your youngster into a star.

Says the mother of a fourteen-year-old daughter: "I had Natalie doing everything in the book—ballet classes, flute lessons, ice-skating lessons, karate. I even found an older kid once to teach her how to juggle. I really wanted her to be good at something that would 'travel,' that would lead her into joining a band or a team or something other kids would admire her for. I think now, looking back, that we spent a lot of money and a lot of time pursuing my agenda, not hers."

Natalie, says her mother, "is at heart a bookworm. Lately, she's become interested in photography and she wants a good camera, which I'll probably get for her. At least this is something she's found for herself."

There's nothing wrong with exposing your child to a variety of lessons and extracurricular activities, and with one child you have more resources available for such pursuits than you would have with a larger family. Many youngsters can enjoy sampling from a smorgasbord of things to learn and do, and many will find an activity that intrigues them.

If your child doesn't object to the lessons or whatever you line up for her, well and good. But keep in mind that fine line between suggesting and promoting, and *pressuring*.

GET YOUR CHILD A PET

Many children love animals, and a pet can make a fine companion for the child without a sibling.

"During Christina's kindergarten year, my stepdaughter Regan, who was nineteen, lived with us for three or four months," says Christina's mother. "On the day Regan left, Christina invented an imaginary kitten. It was amazing. Ten minutes after Glen and Christina and I dropped Regan off at the train station, the imaginary kitten appeared! Christina talked to it, fed it, told her friends at school about it. The kitten stayed with us for about a month, then it faded away."

Although this young child never actually said, "I wish I had a sister," or even, "I wish I had a cat," her parents concluded that she would enjoy a pet, and Christina now has a pair of real-life brother-and-sister kittens to take care of and play with.

Says her mother: "When she went through this period with the imaginary cat after her half-sister left, it didn't seem to me she felt terribly sad or lonely. I think she just had liked the feeling of a bigger family—another warm body around, in a sense, another creature to talk to in a way she didn't talk to her dad and me. And getting a cat was certainly doable as far as we were concerned."

A pet can also provide the only child with regular chores, which is not a bad idea!

GIVE YOUR CHILD CHORES

Several broad-based surveys have indicated this fact: The only child does *fewer* chores than do his siblinged peers.

Many parents who have shared their experiences with us bear out that finding. They admit they've been lax about making their child do work around the house, or they haven't given it much thought at all.

One father was helping his daughter with a fourth-grade project, "My Day," for which each youngster was to describe one day's activities, meals, thoughts, feelings, and so on. "There were checklists for these different categories," says this father, "and one of them was called 'Chores.' Of the ten or twelve items listed there—'I made my bed,' 'I set the table'—there wasn't one thing Sam could say she did. She felt sort of embarrassed. I felt more so, because I realized we never really ask her or expect her to do anything."

Do try to give your child, starting at a young age, some responsibilities for promoting the smooth running of the household. Assign him a few regular chores, according to his age and abilities and what's important to you—helping unpack groceries, picking up toys—and remind him as often as necessary, which will undoubtedly be very often, that this is what he is expected to do.

"It's easier to clear the table and stack the dishwasher myself," says the mother of a young son, "but a while ago we sat down and made a list of all the daily to-do stuff around the house, and he had to pick two or three things that would be his chores. That was one he picked, and I make sure he does it. He's such a little princeling around here, I figure we should see to it that he gets his hands dirty once in a while!"

With one child—and less clutter to clean up, fewer meals to serve, less laundry to fold, than would be true in a larger family—this insisting on the completion of chores can feel a bit false, like make-work projects for the "good" of your child, rather than needed help for the running of the home. Even if it is easier to "do it yourself" and even if you'd prefer to be perpetually pleasant to your child and avoid the taskmaster's voice, make him responsible for some of what needs to get done in the course of a day.

Realizing that even if he is the little princeling he will not always be served is part of that "deflation" process every child needs to grow in a healthy way. Taking part in doing what needs to get done also helps give your child a sense of family involvement. He begins to learn what it feels like to be responsible, on a regular basis, for activities that are vital but not necessarily what he'd like to be doing, and that's a lesson every child needs.

One of the most logical chores is to make your child responsible for keeping his own room in order. His room, in general, should be very much his own territory.

LET YOUR CHILD'S ROOM BE HER SANCTUARY . . . NOT YOUR DREAM

This is her space, and it is appropriate that it reflect aspects of her taste and personality.

Many parents of only children relish the idea of decorating their youngster's room. They want to go overboard for their one and only child; they have, perhaps, the resources with which to indulge those wishes; they want to reinvent and improve upon their own childhood experiences, which may have included handed-down furniture and cramped, shared rooms.

One parent created for her newborn daughter a pastel fantasy of a bedroom. "I had pale-blue, flowered Laura Ashley wallpaper, a canopy over the baby's crib. I had charming old watercolor children's drawings that my grandfather, who was an artist and illustrator, had painted years ago. It was, really, the most unique, peaceful room."

Unhappily for that mother, her little girl began rearranging that lovely haven all too soon. She liked pink and purple. She didn't like the canopy. She wanted a say in what went up on her walls.

You will, of course, set up some general rules about what goes or doesn't go for your youngster's room, but as much as possible, it's good to involve her in the decision making and let her help create her own special child space within the predominantly grown-up atmosphere of her home.

And then help her learn to take care of her own things by making doing so as simple as possible. Specialists in children's furniture and design suggest installing hooks or a peg rack for little children to hang up clothes; they're more likely to do it than if they're expected to fold up pajamas and put clothes in a drawer, for example. Plastic bins with picture labels on the outside to identify the contents are good containers for very young children to use to store drawing supplies or toys.

Some youngsters seem to be natural-born neatniks; some are the exact opposite. It's good to allow a child to enjoy his own space *and* to encourage him to be responsible for keeping it in reasonable working order.

MAKE MEMORIES FROM YOUR SPECIAL ROUTINES AND RITUALS

The word "traditions" has a big sound to it. It suggests big family get-togethers, large numbers of people—all the relatives gathering at Great-Aunt Sally's every Easter for a lavish feast and egg-rolling contests in the backyard. But you really don't need a family of ten to foster and relish the special habits or happenings that make you and your loved ones feel special and unique. Duplicate some happy routines from your own growing-up days in your now much smaller family—they'll still work. Develop new traditions, and remember that they need not be "big ticket" items to be memorable.

"Since becoming a parent myself, I've been very conscious of the things I remember from my own childhood," says one mother. "And they are surprising. I've forgotten about a lot of the 'important' things we did, which my mother is always reminding me about, like taking trips. Or at least I don't have any feelings about them one way or another.

"But I remember vividly that when I was a little girl and my father came home from work, I'd sit on the end of the radiator in the bathroom while he washed his hands and face. I'd be telling him some story, and when I wasn't looking, he'd flick a little water in my face with his fingers. I'd accuse him of this, and he'd look all surprised and say, 'No, no, that wasn't me, that was two other guys!' I adored this routine, which was the same day after day. There was just a great sweetness about it. I felt very close to him.

"Another thing I remember is how much I loved Tuesday evenings, which was my father's bowling night. My mother, brother, and I had dinner without him, and we always had the same thing, which we never had any other night—spaghetti that came in a box with a little can of sauce and a little can of grated cheese. My mother was otherwise very big on meat and vegetables and all. For some reason, this spaghetti dinner always felt cozy and special."

This thoughtful mother of a now eight-year-old boy goes on to express some thoughts that I think will resonate with all readers: "Since having our son, and I think maybe especially because we have just the one and our family is just the three of us, we seem to have become superaware of making family traditions.

"We do a big Christmas tree every year, which my husband and I never did before. We joined a church, so Eric—and we too—would have that sense of community and spiritual life. We give a lot of thought to vacations and providing fun experiences for him to remember. All that is good. But I wonder if maybe what he will remember most fondly are the little, sweet things I hardly notice."

Eric's mother *has* noticed some of the little, sweet things, though. She and Eric have a favorite early Saturday morning routine, in which they sit on the couch under a blanket and watch cartoons while she has her coffee and he has his hot chocolate.

Eric's father started a little wake-up routine years ago. Says Eric's mother: "Bill goes into Eric's room and sings a very dopey song that goes, 'I am Mr. Tuesday, who are you?' while he bounces Eric up and down on the bed. Then he says, 'Dreams, anybody? Any good dream stories this morning?' And anybody who remembers a dream tells it." She thinks Eric is about to outgrow his pleasure in this ritual, but, she says, "The other morning, Bill didn't go in to wake him up as usual, and Eric called, 'Hey, Dad, no Mr. Wednesday this morning?'"

Every child loves the small, unique, repetitive rituals that constitute the rich underpinnings of his own special family.

As you aim for the best for and from your only child, don't forget to enjoy with him the small routines that help to give him a sense of calm, consistency, and continuity.

· 10 ·
A New Look to the American Home

THE ONLY CHILD IN THE SINGLE-PARENT/DIVORCED FAMILY

Jackson's mother and I separated when he was still a baby, and the divorce was over and done with a year later," says the father of an eleven-year-old son. "For ten years, we've had joint custody. When he was still little, he stayed with his mother, and I took him for weekends. Then when he started school we tried doing one week with me, one week at his mother's, but he didn't like that a whole lot. The first few years were rough on everybody, the last few have been more settled. We sort of play it by ear more these days. It's never been what I would call an ideal situation, but my boy is doing great."

Two years after the divorce, Jackson's father married a woman with an older son and daughter from her own first marriage, and subsequently he divorced again. Jackson's mother did not remarry. The parents continued to live near each other and were and are united in their efforts to give their son a normal sense of family life. And Jackson, today an outgoing preadolescent who feels close to both his mom and his dad, seems to be—as his father says—doing great.

In a nutshell, that family's story depicts an increasingly common scenario in late-twentieth-century America. Parents divorce;

their child or children spend their growing years "living" with one parent (in nine out of ten cases, with the mother) and, under custody or visitation or informal arrangements, spending various amounts of time with the parent who is absent from the home. In one decade alone, between 1970 and 1980, the percentage of children aged eighteen or younger living with a single parent jumped from about 12 percent to about 20 percent; even more recent U.S. Census Bureau figures indicate that about a quarter to a third of the nation's families with children are headed by single parents. The largest group of young, divorced mothers comprises women with an only child.

The time leading up to, during, and immediately following a separation or divorce is almost always confusing and difficult, as two adults try to establish two separate, new lives for themselves and, ideally, try to do what is best for their child's or children's well-being. Often—and again ideally—things settle down as time goes on, as any hostilities surrounding the divorce subside and as patterns are established. (Perhaps not surprisingly, some research studies indicate that divorced women with one child have an easier time reorganizing their and their child's lives than do mothers with two or more children. More only-child mothers had been working before the divorce, and more have fewer financial difficulties and fewer child care problems.)

Some divorced parents, like Jackson's father, do remarry. Some of those second marriages bring happiness; some do not—37 percent of remarriages, according to recent demographic studies, end within ten years. Divorce researchers estimate that 15 percent of all children in divorced families will, before they reach age eighteen, see the parent they live with remarry and divorce again.

And like Jackson, many youngsters these days enjoy—or wrestle with—the presence of half-siblings or step-siblings in their lives. Sometimes those children who come along with a father's or mother's remarriage or new living arrangements turn into good playmates and lasting companions. Sometimes they don't—Jackson, for example, no longer sees the stepsister and stepbrother he lived with off and on for almost three years.

In this chapter and the next, we will explore some of the only-child issues that are part of this new look to many American families. As the parent of an only child, you may find yourself somewhere in one of these family constellations. If you are contemplating ending your marriage . . . if you are recently separated or have been divorced for many years . . . if you are struggling with or happy with the custody or visitation arrangements concerning your child . . . if you or your former partner is living in a new family, perhaps one that includes other children . . . you almost surely will experience turbulent and often conflicting feelings. There may be chaos, anger, exhilaration, joy.

And there will be concern about your child.

It can help enormously to step back a bit and consider what's going on in your own emotional life and in your child's during and after the end of a marriage or household—and how those pictures change as time goes on. In this chapter, we'll explore some of the special needs your youngster will have and some of the pitfalls to avoid and possibilities to embrace that will ensure that your child not only adjusts but thrives during the time her family is changing and re-forming.

(Because it's most likely that your youngster is primarily living with her mother while her father has established a separate home elsewhere, most of our examples talk about Mom as the "custodial" parent and Dad as the "absent" parent. That choice is not meant to suggest that other custody arrangements are not viable or that mothers or fathers always come down on one or the other side in the kinds of conflicts or solutions we'll talk about.)

This is a time when your child's "only" status takes on new dimensions—for you (we'll talk later about the natural tendencies of a single parent to form close attachments to her child) and for her. To help her during this time when she does not have a brother or sister or two with whom to share the inevitable adjustments she must make, you should first know just what siblings may provide for each other when the family is disbanding.

DIVORCE AND THE SIBLING FACTOR

It is natural to assume that having a brother or sister or two to share the difficulty of a marital breakup is comforting for a child. As we've said before, the real benefit of siblings is that the household consists of two subgroups, as it were—the children and the grown-ups. Useful when things are running smoothly, that can be especially so when they aren't. During a period of divorce, it's easier for two or more children to separate themselves emotionally from what's going on with the adults—to say, in effect, "Our parents are over there, having their troubles. We're over here, not a part of their troubles."

That can greatly lessen the individual child's tendency to feel he must in some way negotiate or mediate between Mom and Dad. It can also ease his sense of being at fault or responsible for what's happening. All youngsters, no matter how earnestly parents reassure them to the contrary, are sure that they somehow caused their parents' distress. (We'll talk more about that later.) Two or three children can talk to each other about what's going on. Even if they're too young to analyze and verbalize their fears, at least they have each other's comforting presence. Whatever burden of guilt does exist is not all on one child's shoulders.

Judith Wallerstein's long-term study of sixty families that had experienced divorce generally supported the idea that siblings help each other through. Mostly, she found, the children drew closer together and depended on each other more after their parents separated; older children sometimes took it upon themselves to protect or buffer a younger child from the family turmoil.

The sibling factor doesn't always play out in just that way, however. In some cases, Wallerstein found, siblings side with different parents, and that creates animosities or real hatred between brothers and sisters. In another study, conducted among divorced mothers with one, two, and three children, researchers found that the women with two or three rarely indicated that their youngsters had been especially helpful to each other during the stressful time after the divorce. The degree of rivalrous feelings between the siblings and competition for their mother's attentions were factors, as were differences in the way each child felt about his absent father.

This, too, is understandable. Whenever there's a divorce, children become very upset and very angry—and that can mean they don't feel like acting especially nice, even to each other. And while a youngster may not be able to take out the anger on the parent she's living with or on the parent who has left the home, she *can* express all that upset and aggression and disgruntlement toward her kid brother or big sister.

The children may be mean to each other, prone to flare-ups, or even see each other as malevolent, especially if they have different feelings toward their parents or if one child is Mom's favorite and the other is Dad's. (Sometimes, I have found, one or both parents may project a subtle but noticeable attitude that says: This one's my child, that one's your child because he's just like you.)

This is what we can say about the sibling factor during divorce and what you as the parents of an only child should keep in mind: In some families, siblings are deeply comforting to each other; they are loving companions and reassuring presences in each other's lives. They give each other the sustaining feeling that although part of their familiar world is changing, another part remains constant.

In other families, siblings may come out of their respective corners battling away and not be especially helpful, supportive, or even nice to each other, perhaps mirroring hostilities going on between their parents. Unpleasant though they may be for everyone—because the last thing parents or children need is an even higher level of animosity in the household—those sibling battles can serve a useful purpose. They constitute an avenue by which a youngster can express some understandable rage he's carrying around over the collapse of his home.

Often, sibling dynamics during this period of upset undergo a great deal of shifting back and forth between feelings of generosity and antagonism. Your only child will not have either that support, if siblings are close or feeling good about each other, or that acceptable outlet, if siblings are venting their unhappy feelings on each other and absorbing each other's anger. Still, be aware that she's dealing with those difficult feelings all the same, although it may not look that way. It's too scary to get mad at Mom or Dad, and there's no brother or sister around to torment or beat up.

Anger is only one of the uncomfortable emotions your child may experience while all these big changes are taking place in her life. There are other feelings too, for which she will need your special help and attention.

AT THE TIME OF DIVORCE: WHAT YOUR CHILD MAY BE FEELING

If two parents can't get along, dislike each other, and are deeply unhappy in the marriage, they are well advised to divorce. But if you are in that situation, be very aware that your decision is upsetting for your child and be sensitive to what may be going on with him, especially during the early stages of the re-formation of his family.

Not all children, of course, will have all these feelings or reactions. Your child's age is a factor, as is the ease and civility with which you and your partner work out your differences and arrangements for the future. But here is some of what *may* be going on—and how your child might describe his feelings if he could identify and put words to them.

"IT'S MY FAULT."

Your youngster believes she is somehow responsible for what's happening.

Even today, when parents are so enlightened and so aware that they make every effort to convey to a child that the end of a marriage is *not her fault,* she's going to think it is. Especially young children are not sufficiently developed psychologically to realize that they are not central to everything that's going on. An only child already has a heightened sense of being integral to the family relationship and is therefore more likely to see herself as in some way the reason for its dissolution.

It's awful to feel guilty. At the same time, it may actually and paradoxically be somewhat comforting to a child—it may be less scary to feel you've done something bad and you're responsible than to feel helpless and powerless.

"I'VE GOT TO MAKE IT ALL BETTER."

If your youngster is convinced it's all his fault, then he may be equally convinced he must try to fix it up.

The only child is always more likely to be drawn into his parents' lives, when things are going well or not so well; he doesn't identify himself with that "child versus adult" subgroup within the home, because he has no one to build it with. Especially if his parents have always looked upon him as "one of us," if they haven't set up a distinction between child and grown-up, his tendency to get caught up in Mom and Dad's problems is going to be even greater.

Even when parents are not considering divorce but are troubled, the only child might get the idea that he's the one holding them together (and perhaps he is; many parents I have counseled acknowledge that they are staying together because of the child). The youngster may become very good at going back and forth between Mom and Dad, seeing to it in some way that his parents don't argue when he's in the room, or staying out of Mommy's way if she's in a bad mood, or trying to get Daddy to do something that Mommy wants him to do. Even a very young child can feel that he's in the middle and that he must in some way right matters he senses are wrong.

"I DON'T WANT ANYTHING TO CHANGE."

Your child doesn't want what's happening to happen.

I have never seen a youngster who does not wish that his parents would come together again. Even if there was strife and fighting and parents who didn't get along (although not to an extreme, physical, or obviously damaging level), the child still wants his father and mother in the house, everything to remain as it is or go back to what it was, and to make his little way around that situation. When his parents are separating, even if Dad is going to live two blocks away, it can seem to him that his mom and dad have gone to separate parts of the earth.

For the only child, there is a dramatically different feel about the household that has gone suddenly from having three people to having two. He may experience his home as too quiet, too empty, too small. That change is deeply distressing to him.

"I'M WORRIED ABOUT MY MOTHER AND MY FATHER."

He's worried that Mom, who's in the next room, is feeling sad. He's worried that Dad, who's living somewhere else, isn't okay.

The only child, especially, can see himself suddenly as the primary caretaker and watchdog for his parents' well-being. I have observed over and over that when you scratch a little below the surface, the child of parents who are in the throes of divorce feels their unhappiness or loneliness.

The youngster may worry about the parent—typically, the father—who is not there and be concerned about what he's eating or who's fixing dinner for him. He may worry that Dad will never come back. He may know or sense that Mom, whom he's living with, was not happy about the divorce (and divorces rarely occur by mutual agreement), and then perhaps he'll try to be "better" or in other ways become drawn into her emotional life.

"I HAVE TO TAKE MOM'S [OR DAD'S] SIDE."

Your child may suddenly act very protective of you or vehemently defend his other parent against what he perceives as attacks or slights. Even if concerned parents who are divorcing go to pains to encourage their child not to view either of them as the good guy or the bad guy in what's happening, the child may still tend to align himself with one or the other. He may be trying either to assuage his own feelings of fear and vulnerability through assuring himself that one parent anyway will protect him, or to comfort and help the parent he believes is the unhappiest or the most alone.

That sets up for him a distressing dilemma, because even as he feels a need to take Mom's or Dad's side, he senses keenly that he is being disloyal to his other parent. With two (or more) children in the family, that burden of feeling a need to take sides can be shared and lightened.

Again, not *all* children will go through *all* this turmoil *all* the time. But your child will be upset to some degree while the separation or divorce is under way.

Recognize that there is anger and confusion in the air and that those feelings can be overwhelming for your child. Just being aware that she might be struggling at times with one or another of these complex emotions will help you understand specific behaviors and find ways to be reassuring.

And that's so important during a divorce, because just when your child needs you to be especially sensitive to what's going on with her, you are dealing with your own terribly distracting needs and feelings.

AT THE TIME OF DIVORCE: HOW WHAT YOU'RE GOING THROUGH AFFECTS YOUR ABILITY TO BE A PARENT

Each divorce follows its own course, but most divorce counselors agree that the earliest stage—when the decision has been made or is clearly inevitable, when one adult is actually leaving the home— is the toughest for parents and children alike. You may be feeling unhappy or furious or depressed. You and your partner may verbally or even physically fight. You're preoccupied—the end of a marriage is so mentally and emotionally absorbing, even if you've wanted it for ten years. You have feelings specific to your psychology—perhaps a sense of defeat or failure or conflicts over your own aggressiveness. Almost certainly, you're feeling disorganized—even the smallest details in life are being turned upside down.

All that makes it hard to act like a mother or act like a father. Your mind is elsewhere. It creates what Wallerstein terms "the diminished capacity to parent."

Your only child may have school classmates or play-group companions to provide comforting "distractions." At home, he does not have the reassuring presence of another child who is sharing his experiences.

Try to make life easier for your youngster during this time of change:

PLAY WITH YOUR CHILD, TALK TO YOUR CHILD

That may be the last thing you feel like doing sometimes, as you're adjusting to your own new life and preoccupied with your needs. One single mother, a teacher, remembers that in the weeks after her husband moved out, she wanted "nothing more than to be left alone. I'd come home from school and I was wiped out, and that was always when Liza would pounce on me. Sometimes I completely lost it, and I'd scream at her to just let me alone."

Remember that the loss of parent-child contact time can be one of the most immediate and difficult fallouts for a youngster when the two-parent household breaks up. The custodial parent spends less time with her, because of increased outside pressures, returning to work or school or moving from a part-time to a full-time job, or other preoccupations; the absent parent sees the child in concentrated but limited increments of time.

Set aside special one-on-one times with your child—a talk or a round of Candyland before bedtime, a couple of hours in the park on a Friday afternoon—when you will be totally focused on her.

STAY IN TOUCH WITH THE GRANDPARENTS OR THE FAVORITE AUNT AND COUSINS

The mother of a boy who was six at the time of his parents' separation says that for several months afterward, Mark talked repeatedly about his cousins and other relatives. "It seemed he was constantly 'counting his kin.' He'd ask me, and we'd go down the list all over again. I'd say, That's right, you have four grandparents, you have three aunts and one uncle, you have three cousins, and so on. I think being an only child had something to do with the need he had to reassure himself that even though his father wasn't right there anymore, he still had a family."

Mark's mother set up a lot of visits with those relatives, which she says was good for her as well as for her son, because "it helped diffuse some of the tension in the family atmosphere." Relatives—and adult friends as well—often don't know what to say or don't want to appear to take sides. Reduce the sense of social isolation that may have descended on both you and your child by maintaining or increasing family contacts where you can.

KEEP UP FAMILIAR ROUTINES

There are many big changes happening in your life and thus in your child's. His world feels more unstable than it used to. He'll find a lot of comfort now in the fact that you still wake him up in the morning with a little tussle or you still have pizza every Friday dinner or you still put him to bed by saying, "Night, night, don't let the bedbugs bite."

It is hard during this unraveling time in your own life to remain sensitive to your child's smallest needs—enough, you might say, that you're getting him dressed and fed and to school on time. But keeping up little routines is more important than ever.

DON'T LET HIM GET AWAY WITH MURDER

That "diminished capacity to parent" can include an unwilling-ness—or lack of energy or strength—to discipline and keep established rules and regulations going. I have found that when children are first coming to grips with the changes that divorce brings, they may become either unusually quiet, docile, and "good," in an effort to help their parent *and* to keep themselves protected, or unusually rambunctious, ornery, and "difficult," in an attempt to get attention and from a need to vent feelings.

Perhaps now more than ever, disciplining your child will try your patience and sap the energy that you don't think you have. But maintaining rules—yes, you do have to brush your teeth; no, you are not allowed to kick; yes, you do have to put the garbage out when I ask you to; no, you cannot watch TV if your home-work isn't done—is another way to keep a familiar tone to the home and to help him feel more secure.

Your child may feel scared when he knows he's *out* of control and realizes Mom or Dad isn't *in* control.

DON'T USE YOUR CHILD TO GARNER INFORMATION ABOUT WHAT HIS OTHER PARENT IS UP TO

Especially in the early stage of divorce, while emotions are still so raw and change is still so new, it can be very tempting to quiz your youngster when she comes back from a visit with her absent parent. One mother says her son's offhand remark that his father had bought a new couch "led me off on a string of questions: What color? Where did he get it? Was it a pull-out? It must have sounded like a grilling. Finally, my son said, 'Why do you care anyway?' I didn't know why. In fact, I really didn't care, so why was I doing this?"

Two siblings arriving home from a visit with their absent parent will find it easier than will the only child to "escape," if they wish, a mother who seems to be lying in wait to find out details of a weekend they may not feel like talking about right away.

It's normal to be curious about your former partner's new life, new girlfriend or boyfriend, new home. But it's wrong for a parent to involve a child in any way in the parents' business—it need not even be as serious as spying or asking for information on a girlfriend.

I have often observed that though parents are divorced, things are still not settled between them. Closure hasn't come, or it hasn't come on both sides; there's still fuel there, still angry feelings or a need to get back at the other. As a therapist, I have sometimes seen a parent who, even two, three, or more years after the divorce, has not finished with it all. As soon as he or she starts talking about the ex-mate, pow! It's back to square one in terms of expressions of anger.

How long that closure and finishing process takes varies,

depending on the couple and the circumstances. When there's a child, of course, it's harder to bring the marital relationship to a conclusion, because two adults have to keep talking about child-related issues. Even then, there should be a gradual diminution of that intensely emotional content, and eventually even the resentments and the anger should die out. It depends on each person's strengths and determination to get on with life, and it may take some hard work to accept that the relationship is really finished.

During these early weeks and months, when you're probably still very far from viewing your ex-spouse unemotionally, monitor yourself to be sure you are not using your child in big or even small ways to play out any resentments you may be having. It's damaging to say to a child, for example, "No, Dad can't come tonight, he'd rather go to a party," or, "Oh, your father took you *there*? If you didn't want to go, you should have said no. Why can't you talk up to him?" On a psychological level, that child is still helping his parents finish their battles.

Over time—a year or two or more—things settle down, emotions fade, both grown-ups and child become caught up in their changed lives, finances (usually) become more stable. Be conscious of what your child is feeling and needing during the bumpy passage.

Of course, perhaps the most critical piece of business that must be worked out early on and that will continue until your child reaches the late teenage years is custody and visitation arrangements.

ONE CHILD, TWO HOUSEHOLDS

As much as your child may love to and long to see her father (most commonly, as we have said, it's Dad who is living elsewhere) and as determined as both adults may be to keep that vital relationship alive and well, visitations are not always going to be pleasant and strain-free.

Siblings can play a useful role for each other in helping to make visitations with the absent parent comfortable and pleasurable. One mother, divorced for seven years, with a now seventeen-year-old daughter and ten-year-old son, says: "Aaron and Marie have spent every other weekend and half of all school holidays with their dad, always together. Marie has always been a 'little mother' type to Aaron, and especially when they were younger, I know she made it really easy for him in little ways to be at his dad's home. She knew things like he wanted to sleep with his Luke Skywalker power sword and so on. It's harder to keep to our schedule these days, but both kids still really do want to go together to their father's. They're there for each other."

A sibling can be a comfort or buffer, a familiar presence that the only child doesn't have as he adjusts to the inevitable strangeness of living in two households. And no matter how lovingly the absent parent tries to make his youngster feel at home, there will be strangeness and adjustments to make. Even when mother and father are having a tranquil post-divorce working out of things, even when they're happy to be divorced and living their own lives, even when both adults are united in their plans for raising their youngster, it is still the *child* who is put in the position of having to do all the accommodating. It is the *child* who must deal with the aftermath of all the nonsense that went on between her parents.

Mom says, This weekend you're going to Dad's—and perhaps the youngster is looking forward to seeing her father or at least is very dutiful about going. But there's *nothing natural* about these arrangements for the child; it hasn't anything to do with her life. It's no easier or more comfortable for her than it would be for you or me to live three days a week in one place and four in another, or to spend one weekend here and one weekend there.

In a sense, the child will always be in a state of some rebellion over the arrangements, and with some youngsters, that state can create internal havoc—especially since rarely can a child articulate or acknowledge to herself what's going on and even more rarely will she feel she can express it.

I say this not to scare you but to urge you to remember that your child, without the possible reassurance or at least the company of a brother or sister, is being asked, in effect, to establish two separate lives in two separate places, and that's not appealing. What's most important in easing the process is that you and your former spouse keep talking to each other as parental allies, keep comparing notes on what is going on with your youngster, and keep a willingness to reassess and realign arrangements as he develops and as his needs change (more later on that score).

TRANSITIONS, TOYS, TV, AND MORE

Here are some specific thoughts on how to ensure comfort for a young only child:

BOTH PARENTS SHOULD BE ON HAND DURING DROP-OFF AND PICK-UP TIMES

Transition times—when your child is leaving for the weekend at Dad's or is coming back to Mom's after a few days away—can be unsettling for your child. Packing up and leaving can feel like starting all over. If at all possible, both parents should be present when those switches are being made.

TALK TO YOUR EX-SPOUSE ABOUT THE CURRENT DETAILS OF YOUR CHILD'S LIFE

Put it in a note if you find talking impossible. Especially if your child is very young, each parent must know about changes in nap times, food preferences, or when a youngster is getting over a cold or suddenly must have the stuffed lion to sleep with. Remember there is no sibling on hand to do the reminding.

TALK TO YOUR EX-SPOUSE ABOUT HIS PLANS FOR YOUR CHILD'S WEEKEND AWAY

Then you can let your youngster know that *you* know what's coming up, and you can help her feel that her two separate lives are part of one whole picture.

TRY VERY HARD TO REACH COMPROMISES WITH YOUR EX-SPOUSE ABOUT BEDTIME, TV TIME, AND MEALTIME

Very frequently, I have found, parents battle about what the custodial parent feels is the absent parent's laxness in sticking to rules regarding those most ticklish subjects.

The mother of seven-year-old Megan says: "On the one hand, I understand it. Frank sees his kid one afternoon and evening during the week and then every other weekend, and when she goes with him he wants to get as much of her as possible and also, maybe, hates to be the disciplinarian. Also, it's the weekend, and she doesn't have to get up for school. So in my house she's in bed by eight, and at his place, she's up on Friday and Saturday until midnight, watching Marx Brothers movies with her father. For dinner, they always go out to a fast-food place, which of course she loves and which I don't approve of. So he and I are constantly arguing about all this."

The absent parent of an only child, more readily than would a father who's looking out for two youngsters, may be inclined to let rules go by the board. With just one, there's less mess, less to get done, no sibling squabbles that would incline Dad to take a harder line about bedtimes and the rest.

Children will survive on fast-food dinners and some bent rules about TV and bedtime, but when parents are consistently very far apart in agreement over these matters and regularly get into fights about them, that's a source of distress for the child.

GIVE YOURSELF AND YOUR YOUNGSTER TIME TO SETTLE IN WHEN SHE RETURNS HOME

Don't pepper her with questions about her weekend away; she may want to be quiet, get readjusted, and just spend an hour or so "feeling" the comfortable presence of her familiar room.

And you need to ease rather than jump back into your own parent self. One woman describes it this way: "When Jeffrey is off with his father, I do *my* thing. I have some girlfriends over, and we throw together a dinner. I do my workouts. I take baths. I'm totally out of the mother mode. Then my son comes home, and I have to get reoriented."

Give yourselves an hour or two, or as long as it takes to get reacclimated. The information you might want to hear about your child's time away will come out gradually.

DON'T MAKE ANY BIG CHANGES IN HOME BASE WHILE YOUR CHILD IS AWAY

One mother used the week when her son was vacationing with his father to redecorate the boy's room. The changes were minor, really—a new bedspread and matching curtains. When the boy returned to his mother's home, he was deeply upset about this new look and insisted that the old items be returned. Another young child burst into tears when she discovered that her mom had thrown out a very old, withered corn plant that had been standing in the living room. She talked about the missing plant for a week.

What those little children were saying, I suspect, is: I don't want any more changes. It happened once. I don't want it to happen again. I want to know that everything is going to remain the same from now on.

Remember that the first context of a child's world is: This is Mommy, this is Daddy, this is my house. Now that context has changed, and he wants the secure sense that even if all *that* is not going to remain the same, at least he knows his table and toy chest and bedspread are going to be the way he left them. An only child, especially, often has a strong emotional investment in his room and in familiar items. It's a deep need to know where he is! Then, from a securely felt home base, he can branch out.

None of this is easy if anger between you and your ex-spouse is still running high and when both parents are still focused on and absorbed by their own situations. Complicating the picture is the fact that the absent parent, who isn't spending as much daily time around the child, may not be as adept at keeping things going; the youngster may feel a little awkward in that parent's home.

But the most important factor in how happily your child will adjust to your arrangements is the way that you two adults work together and trust each other as parents.

OVER THE YEARS: KEEPING A CUSTODY AGREEMENT VIABLE

A three-year-old is helping Mom pack up her knapsack for a visit with her father and thinking: Hooray, I'm going to spend time with Daddy! I can't wait until he gets here.

A six-year-old bitterly resents not being able to see his friends in the park on Saturday and would rather skip the weekend visit.

A thirteen-year-old who's always adored the times she spent

with her father suddenly feels shy and self-conscious staying over at his house, with just the two of them there.

A fifteen-year-old hates the summer plans his mother has lined up and wants to spend his school vacation living with his dad and helping out in his shop.

As we explored in the chapter on the family threesome and triangulation, your child, as he develops from age one up to the time he heads off for college, is normally going to have different feelings about which parent he wants to be with at which times. It does *not* necessarily have anything to do with problems in the parent/child relationship. Even within intact family threesomes, these shifts and preferences take place: the youngster says, "I only want to go to the park today with Mommy!" or, "I want Dad to read me a story, not you."

Your youngster will sometimes want to align herself with one parent or the other, depending on what developmental stage she is in, what her current (often shifting) feelings are about Mom or Dad, and what is going on in her life outside the family. Once she starts to get a tiny feeling or a big, strong feeling that she *really* doesn't want to go to the absent parent's house every weekend or she *really* would like to spend more time there than she's "allowed" to, she feels guilty and in conflict, and that can make for a lot of internal turmoil.

That's why I firmly believe that parents mustn't think that a custody and visitation agreement decreed at one year of age should remain absolutely the same at twelve years of age . . . or that the child should be the one who must always stay on the program. Parents must not say, "Well, we've made the arrangement now; you'll spend every other weekend and every Wednesday night with your father, and there it is." A child's mind and needs will be changing from year to year or even from month to month.

To be sensitive to those changing needs takes a great deal of parental resolve, intelligence, control, and maturity. It is not easy, even when both parents want what's best for their child, if one parent is feeling out of favor or is fearful of losing touch with the youngster. I have often heard a father say: I want to be with my child, I want to be in the loop, and if I accede to this and say, Okay, you won't come to my house right now, then I won't have a relationship with him.

Those feelings are inevitably more intense for the only child's parents. With two or perhaps three children, the chances are that each youngster's developmental stages and preferences will be different at any given time; if one child feels like "abandoning" Dad or Mom for a while, another child may happen to be feeling particularly close to Dad or Mom right then.

IN MY OFFICE: WHAT I TELL PARENTS

In my practice, I frequently counsel divorcing parents who are in the middle of the upheaval and seeking help in working out arrangements concerning their child. This, in essence, is what I tell them:

"Once the arrangements are settled, it is probably best for your child at the beginning to get into the routine of the back-and-forth visits. Establish a pattern and a structure. It's not good to leave it up to the *child* every week, asking, 'Do you want to be at Daddy's or Mommy's this week?' or whatever. That puts the child in a terrible bind.

"Once the arrangement is in place and the wrinkles have been ironed out, *be very attentive* over time to how well it's continuing to work. If it starts to feel that what you're asking of your child is untoward—'No, you can't see your friends this weekend'; 'No, you can't stay home, you must go even if you don't want to'—then be open to exploring what adjustments might be made in the structure.

"This is the arrangement you have agreed upon right now, but I hope you can continue to work with each other and with me throughout your child's development, so that we can reevaluate it at every stage. If it becomes clear that your youngster is temporarily at a place developmentally where she doesn't want to stay at her mother's house or at her father's house, I hope that you will be able to listen to those signals, that we can talk it over, and that you can let your child be where she wants to be. I hope you will be able to explore what alternatives are possible. Perhaps parent and child can meet for early dinners two or three times a week or do one nice thing together on a weekend afternoon—getting together for small increments of time more often might be most comfortable for your child during that particular phase.

"Don't take it as a personal rejection. Children shift back and forth all the time. As long as the relationship between each of you and your child is basically solid, you'll be fine. A year later, she'll want to spend time with the other parent. But when she's forced to do something she really doesn't want to do, you're in trouble.

"Stay open to her developmental needs. Then you are accommodating her; she is not accommodating some fixed arrangement that no longer is best for her. You'll be in much better shape in your relationship with your child, and she will be in much better shape."

REARRANGING THE ARRANGEMENT: STEPS TO TAKE

To know when and if it's time to do a little rethinking of custody or visitation arrangements:

TAKE REGULAR SOUNDINGS ON YOUR CHILD

Listen to what's going on and to what she's saying. If you are well tuned in to your youngster, you will be able to distinguish between a little "I just don't feel like going" grousing or a little "I know Mom wants to go away for the weekend, and I'm in the mood to give her a little grief right now," and feelings that reflect a deep need or wish.

Does your child look in any way as if he's really suffering over the stated plans? Perhaps he's too compliant, goes off too quietly and readily, doesn't say much about it—but suddenly you hear that he's daydreaming at school, isn't getting work done, isn't really on top of things.

Perhaps, week after week, you and your child go through a tortured routine of "I don't want to go," "Yes, I do want to go," "No, I don't," accompanied by a lot of dallying over getting the bag packed and so on.

Perhaps, week after week, there are somatic complaints when it's time to switch households—"I have a stomachache," "I don't feel well," "My head hurts"—which are saying: Mom's going to rescue me here, because she's the one who takes care of aches and pains.

The signs will be there, and if they are present repeatedly and excessively, your child is not happy with the arrangement.

TALK TO AN INFORMED AND NEUTRAL THIRD PARTY

Reassessing custody and visitation is one situation where it is enormously helpful, I would say vital, to talk as a couple to an outside third party—a psychologist, social worker, school guidance counselor, minister, or some other person who is professionally oriented, who understands the issues, and who can help you gauge what's going on with your child.

Often, it is not necessary to have more than one or two sessions. In my practice, I see many parents who come in once every year or two, just to touch base and see that things are on course. A counselor can help you distinguish among those temporary "I want to give Mom some grief this weekend" moods and shifting developmental stages or other significant concerns.

Talking to that third-party advocate for your child can be especially helpful if you and your ex-spouse are really at odds or finding it impossible to hear each other out, or if one parent finds it difficult to detach his own wishes from his child's needs.

Only children, as we have said, are always more likely than children with siblings to become drawn into parents' lives. And when parents are divorced or not living together, it's especially easy for a mother or father or both to treat their youngster as something *more* than a son or daughter.

In this next section, let's explore:

PITFALLS FOR THE SINGLE PARENT: THE ONLY CHILD AS COMFORTER, CONFIDANT, PAL

A parent who loses a mate to divorce—who loses the other adult half of the triangle—tends unconsciously to cause the child to "rise" in age. That youngster becomes "older" or more adult in the parent's perception, and that can happen for perfectly appropriate reasons.

When parents are caught up in the busyness and perhaps confusion of establishing two homes, when one or both adults are more than usually pressured for time or concerned about finances, there can be a parent/child "we're in this together" feeling in the air. The youngster instinctively may sense that he must "grow up" a bit faster in one way or another, assume greater responsibility for the smooth running of the households and for his own comfort. For example, studies have shown that only children in single-parent homes do more chores—and with less nagging from Mom or Dad—than do only children in intact homes.

There can be absolutely nothing wrong with this; children can thrive and grow stronger when they mature in these ways. Problems may arise, however, when either parent looks to the youngster to satisfy most of his or her own needs for warmth, affection, and companionship.

Here's how that may happen—the three most common ways single parents of only children may tend to blur the line between adult and child:

THE ONLY CHILD AS COMFORTER

"She considers me to be her best friend. She tells me so," says the divorced mother of an eight-year-old daughter. "And it's very seductive to be her best friend. My relationship with her can be very consuming, very fulfilling. She likes to sleep in my bed with me, and I think: Well, why not? What's the harm? There she is, so cute, so adorable, so crazy about me. Better than a man in many ways!

"I do see there can be a danger in our being so attached. I ask myself if I'm letting this child fill in all the gaps in my own life. I'm not married, not seeing anyone. My life right now is really my daughter and my job."

It is often difficult and even painful for a divorced parent, especially in the early years after the end of the marriage, to jump back into the fray and pursue new romantic relationships or even adult friendships. Opportunities for socializing may be limited by time and money as well as emotional constraints. I have counseled single parents who feel, as this mother does, that there's simply no energy or desire left over for a life beyond being a wage earner and being a parent.

Certainly do allow yourself to take comfort from the presence of your child. To some extent, it's expectable that a degree of the intensity you experienced in your relationship with your former spouse will be transferred to your youngster. But do also be very conscious—as this mother is coming to be—that you do not allow your child to fill in all the gaps in your own life. Over time, that kind of dependency can be damaging on both sides.

THE ONLY CHILD AS CONFIDANT

"I am certain that part of the trouble between Krista and me had to do with the fact that she's an only child and I'm a single parent," says the mother of a teenage daughter whose problems with her mom reached such an explosive level that Krista moved out to live, at least temporarily, with a friend's family.

"I told her everything that was going on all the time, told her what was wrong with her father, told her what I did or didn't like about my boyfriend. This was dumb and wrong, but she was always so sympathetic, and she actually had good advice. And she always just seemed to sense how I was feeling at any time. We were so thick, it was almost inevitable there would be a split."

I have seen over and over in my practice how tempting it can be for the divorced parent to make the only child of the same sex his or her peer or confidant, as did Krista's mother. (It can happen in multichild families, too, that the parent will designate one child, depending on age and personality, as the one to "pull her along" emotionally or to confide in.) And children are so terrific these days! They're smart, they're on top of things, they *do* make good companions.

That kind of emotional chumminess might be especially likely to happen between a mother and daughter, and especially if the daughter is, say, nine or ten or older. Girls tend to feel themselves more responsible for how Mom is doing and appoint themselves guardians of their parent's emotional well-being.

Both parent and child can benefit from that intimacy and mutual dependency, *as long as it doesn't go too far.* Certainly it would seem in Krista's case, as her mother now acknowledges, that a pattern of Mom's excessively and inappropriately confiding in her daughter led the teenager to attempt to end those intense connections. But although emotions are turbulent between them now, Krista's splitting off may turn out to be beneficial for both in the long run.

When adolescence is going along seemingly as smoothly as can be, when mother and daughter or father and son are telling each other their romantic problems, or when one parent is talking to the child about his or her continuing difficulties with the other parent, the child really does not have the opportunity to rebel. She doesn't break away and move toward independence because, first, she may not feel free to be rebellious, and second, she may find this kind of closeness and sharing with her parent very gratifying. She may feel she can talk to no one as she can to her mother—and that's not a good sign.

When a child normally and healthily breaks away, when that adolescent rebellion has come and gone and the child has moved successfully into her own young-adult life, she then indeed may come around to concluding, "Gee, when it's all said and done, there really is no one like my mother to talk to." But it's a very different thing when the child is going through the major developmental stages in which she needs to be separating from her parents and investing in her peers, and needs to build relationships with boys, learning to trust and make emotional commitments. Then to be relied on as confidant by a parent can constitute a destructive reversal of roles.

Do enjoy your child's companionship, but don't make her your girlfriend or make him your buddy. Because she's an only and not part of a "child subgroup" in the family, that kind of crossing the line between parent and child reverberates more strongly, with more potentially unhealthy consequences.

THE ONLY CHILD AS PAL

Separated parents frequently reveal this bone of contention: the custodial parent feels she's the designated bad guy and disciplinarian, while the absent parent is there for the child's sheer enjoyment.

Margaret, the mother of eleven-year-old Max, describes it

this way: "The biggest issue between Larry and me over the whole seven years that we've been divorced is me having to deal with day-to-day problems and him arriving on weekends to be the savior.

"When Max sees his father, it's all fun and games," Margaret continues "They do things together. They rent movies, while Max wouldn't be caught dead watching a movie with me, and that was true even when he was younger. It's all I can do to get him to come and eat with me. But when he's with Larry, he's totally with Larry. Maybe it's partly our personalities, but I think a lot of it is because Larry doesn't get into 'You have to clean your room,' 'You have to get dressed and get out.' In my experience, the parent the kid isn't living with is the doll!"

Often, I have found, when the two children of divorced parents spend their weekend or their school break with their absent parent, normal routines are maintained. The youngsters tend to "hang out" together, watch TV, or play games. When siblings can entertain each other, Dad probably doesn't unconsciously feel the need to provide so much "fun" himself. And as we have observed, with more than one child to care for and keep track of, he may be more inclined to stick to rules about mealtimes, bedtimes, and cleanups.

When the absent parent—typically, the father—sees his child perhaps once or twice a week and on every other weekend, they may pass less time together than they did when the family was intact. Or a father may in fact be spending the same number or even a greater number of hours with his youngster. Whatever the quantity, the quality of that time between the parent and his child almost inevitably changes. There may be guilt on the father's part that circumstances have separated him from most of his child's daily life, or there may be deep longing to connect with his youngster in only the happiest ways. There may indeed be a wish to be seen as the "good guy," the partner in fun.

As the parent of an only, you will of course tend to focus on your child when you're with her, and if you're with her only on certain days of the week or weeks of the year, you will of course want your time together to be as pleasurable as possible. But it's not best for the needed balance among grown-ups and child for parents always to play out "good cop/bad cop" roles, for one always to be the rule giver and the other always the fun giver. That can add to the tendency of the child of divorced parents to feel conflicted between the two.

As you and your ex-spouse forge a new shape to your own and your child's lives, you'll make the right decisions as long as you remember what we have called the fundamental equation of the only-child family: You are the adults, your child is the child and is growing.

Those realities take on more complexity if you and your ex-spouse find new partners and your child is required to adapt to the presence of new "parents" and "siblings" in his life.

· 11 ·
Step-Siblings, Half-Siblings

When Your Only Child Isn't Quite an Only Anymore

Navigating the waters of divorce in ways that help your only child survive a wrenching change and go on to thrive in his divided family takes parental effort, clear-sightedness, and fortitude. More of those qualities are called for if you or your ex-spouse or both of you go on to remarry and live with a partner who already had children and/or you thereupon produce a child or two of your own.

For a parent, that amounts to getting on with a new life, one you hope to find happier and more satisfying. For the only child, becoming part of a new "blended family" can be something else entirely.

When a parent remarries and starts a new family, or becomes a stepparent to someone else's children, the only child acquires a new presence in her life—a "brother" or "sister" or two. Over the long run, many half- and step-sibling relationships grow into loving connections for the children involved. In the short run, those sudden intruders in the only child's life can cause resentment and confusion. They can throw him for a loop!

BLENDING FAMILIES: DILEMMAS FOR CHILD AND PARENTS

Two divorced mothers who talked to us for this book shared stories about their only children that clearly reveal some of the issues that can be troublesome.

"Angela's father and I separated when she was seven months old, so I never had a plan or special hope for another child," says Patricia, the mother of a six-year-old daughter. "Her father remarried a few years ago and now has a one-year-old son, so Angela has recently gained a half-brother. She sees her dad every other weekend, as she has all along, which worked out fine until the baby came along.

"Things haven't been going too well lately. I see the whole situation as simple sibling rivalry, and her understandable puzzlement and resentment at this new person taking up so much attention. And where does she fit in with her dad and his wife and now the baby?

"But he sees it—and I know this, because we've had a major blowup over this issue—as me somehow turning her against the baby. She comes home and tells me, 'Dad says I have to be nicer to Simon. I *am* nice. I just don't care about him.'"

Angela's mother is mainly concerned that her youngster maintain a steady contact with her father and feel comfortable and wanted during her time with him. Angela's father no doubt wants that too, but he is also enmeshed in the preoccupations of his new life, new wife, and new baby.

Laura, the mother of Ben, now twenty years old, tells a somewhat similar story. After Ben's parents were divorced, his father, Steve, remarried—and later divorced—a woman with two sons around Ben's age. The boys had no contact with their biological father, who lived in another country. "Steve's new wife was determined that Steve would be a father to her children and give them the attention, affection, and support he gave his own son," says Laura.

"Steve felt, I think, that he constantly had to prove to her that he wasn't favoring Ben over her kids. As a result, he seemed to give Ben short shrift. For example, sometimes he'd cancel visits with him to take his stepsons somewhere. Also, Ben slept on a cot in the basement of their house, while the other kids had their own rooms. When I complained, Steve always said I was being over-protective."

Complicating the picture, the three boys were "often butting heads when they were together," says Laura. "I gathered from what my ex-husband and my son told me over the years that when Ben wasn't there, things went smoothly with Steve's step-sons. Then Ben entered the picture off and on, and there were constant frictions among the three of them. They all got touchy about little things, like who would be first to get homework help from Steve."

Steve has always loved his son and been close to him, says Laura, but she feels that in that household the growing boy felt like the odd man out. The "real children" were those youngsters who had their own rooms and seemed to have most of his father. Ben now tells his mother that he tried to make brothers out of his two step-siblings, but it didn't really work. "Perhaps if he had had a sibling of his own," says his mother, "he would have felt he had someone on his side."

ON GAINING A HALF- OR STEP-SIB: HOW YOUR CHILD MAY FEEL

If all goes well over time, as apparently it did not in Ben's case, blended sibling relationships may turn out fine. But initially, they invariably require difficult adjustments for the only child. This is a monumental change in her life, which may involve some painful feelings:

SHE FEELS NOT SO SPECIAL ANYMORE

Whatever else an only child may be, she maintains a special status with her parents simply because she's the only one of her kind in the home or homes she lives in. When another child who has an intimate connection with one of her parents enters her life, sometimes quite suddenly, she may be hurt, puzzled, resentful, or angry that she's not quite the one and only any longer.

That, of course, is what happens when married parents produce baby number two, but the "dethronement" of the once only child may play itself out more naturally or comfortably within an intact family foursome.

The youngster who is feeling miffed or jealous because Mom is spending all her time with the baby and seems to love the baby more may get clingy and demanding of more attention. And then Mother, seeing the need to make her firstborn feel a little special again, provides some extra hugging or holding. Or that youngster who is feeling miffed with Mother can decide to go and snuggle up to Dad for a while and feel special again.

All those small behaviors by which the once only child gradually gets herself adjusted to a new brother or sister (and to the realization that she is not special any longer in quite the way that she once was) are inevitably more strained or constrained when they happen in two different homes and with a new "parent" on the scene. Loving and understanding connections between a stepparent and stepchild can develop, but seldom quickly or easily. The only child who was once so special to two parents may not be quite sure now where she fits within this bigger and more complicated picture.

SHE MAY FEEL ABANDONED

The only child of divorced parents, much more so than typically does a child with siblings, becomes used to sharing many daily activities with Mom or Dad. A parent's remarriage can bring an end to that kind of easy togetherness in small ways the parent may not even notice.

Eleven-year-old Allyson remembers how she and her mother liked to spend Friday or Saturday evening "pigging out with popcorn in front of the TV. Before that, we'd do the laundry together and talk a lot when we were folding clothes and putting stuff away." Recently, her mother married a man she had been seeing for several years, whose nine-year-old daughter from a previous marriage lives with them for part of each week.

Now the Friday evening laundry-and-popcorn routine and other small mother/daughter moments don't happen very frequently. Although the two girls get along "okay," says Allyson, "my mother thinks Jeannie and I should do things together while she and my stepfather do things together." Unconsciously, Allyson's mother relegated her daughter too thoroughly to the new "child subgroup" within the home, and Allyson felt a keen sense of loss and abandonment.

SHE HAS TO SHARE SPACE AS WELL AS ATTENTION

Whether an only child has a lavish bedroom filled with toys or a tiny alcove big enough for a bed and bureau, it's all his. He has become quite comfortable with not only his own "things" but his own "space" as well. Many only children, as we have seen, relish and derive satisfaction from their solitary pursuits, from the time and quiet afforded them in a household without other children.

Suddenly spending part of their lives in close association with a step-sibling or half-sibling is jarring.

SHE IS ABRUPTLY, PERPLEXINGLY, EXPECTED TO BE MORE GROWN-UP

As we've noted, as soon as a second child is born, the parents very commonly perceive their firstborn as suddenly much "older." Where previously they had considered a two-and-a-half-year-old their baby, now she's the "big girl" or he's the "big boy," and in various small ways they convey to that child that they expect more grown-up behavior.

If your only child suddenly has a baby half-sibling in her life, she may take those "big girl" remarks very much to heart and try hard to act in the more mature ways her parent seems to want from her. She may become a "little angel" and not allow herself to acknowledge, even to herself, any of the unhappiness she feels at being dethroned from her exclusive position in Dad's eyes. In the process, she may quash some of her natural joyousness and spontaneity.

Or she may bitterly and actively resent what feels like pressure to grow up faster. She doesn't *want* to and isn't ready to, and she hates the baby who seems to be the cause of those feelings.

HOW TO HELP YOUR ONLY CHILD MAKE THE BEST OF IT, GET THE MOST FROM IT

When sibling rivalries, a new part-time parent, and other startling developments become part of your child's life, she will benefit from your compassionate guidance—which I would best characterize as helping her face reality. She may not like the new order of things (you may not either). But she must be made to understand, first of all, that it is there to stay. And then she must be helped to appreciate what is expected of her and what responsibilities she has in her new families.

TALK FRANKLY ABOUT THE SITUATION

Encourage your child to try to understand her other parent's new life. With a very young child, it's good to review just what has happened. Divorce always has difficult effects for a youngster, and a parent's remarriage and new family might again stir up confusions and wishes that she could somehow undo the divorce and have everything back the way it was. She will feel better when she's reminded that it certainly wasn't her fault and that she certainly does have a place in the new life each parent is forming.

Angela's mother might say to her daughter something like this: "Your dad and I didn't get along well. It was our trouble. We had to get a divorce, and once we did, it meant we were no longer married. We had to make a very hard decision, and we spent a lot of time figuring out how we could both see you as much as possible, because we both love you very much.

"Now he and I are making new lives, separate from each other, but we both want you to be part of those new lives. Maybe you and I can both be happy for Daddy, that he has this new family and that he doesn't have to live by himself. And maybe when the new baby gets a little older, you can show him how to do all the things you know how to do that he will have to learn."

Angela's mother must summon up enough generosity—and not be so furious with her former husband that bitterness and resentment take over—to help her child through by supporting *him*. She needs to do what she can to foster a continuing connection with the absent parent.

GIVE YOUR CHILD A LITTLE GREATER CONTROL

Especially if your child is still quite young, he is bound to be feeling a bit out of control, at least temporarily, about the situation he finds himself in. Let him make his own decisions where he can— what he'll wear in the morning or eat for dinner that night—as a way of giving him hope, encouraging him to feel not so helpless about what's going on in his world.

MAKE CLEAR WHAT YOUR CHILD HAS TO TOLERATE

In the broadest terms, that can be simply stated: Daddy's new baby and new wife or Mommy's new husband and his son or daughter are not going to go away.

If a child returns from a visit with her absent parent and new family full of miseries and complaints, or perhaps sullen and unhappily silent, it can be easy to feel all "on your child's side." It is tempting to shower her with sympathy—and thus convey a message that her feelings take predominance over anything else in the picture.

The once only child who gains a sibling within an intact family learns a painful reality lesson in little stages day by day: They're not going to give the baby back! This kid is here to stay! For your only child, that reality may be harder to accept, because in fact that other child or children *may* "go away," may *not* be right there every minute of every day.

Try to stay tuned in to your own responses to your youngster, and keep a healthy balance between letting her know you sympathize and letting her know she has some responsibilities, too, in making herself happy and in promoting the smooth running of both her families.

ENFORCE WHATEVER RULES YOU AND YOUR EX-SPOUSE (IDEALLY) HAVE AGREED UPON OR HOLD IMPORTANT

It can be especially uncomfortable for you at this time, as you watch your child perhaps struggling to make her own uncomfortable accommodations to the new order of things in her young life, to stick to your guns about rules and regulations. It can take effort, because ideally you will work *with* your ex-spouse in keeping clear-eyed, united, and consistent about what you want from your child and what is good for her.

But she needs that structure in her life, so let your youngster know very clearly what behaviors are expected of her, and that there will be consequences if she doesn't live up to them. Those rules may have to do with sticking to bedtimes and TV-viewing times, doing homework, or whatever else you have determined is what you want to happen.

It may also be helpful right now to see how you might encourage a little attitude improvement, should that seem called for. If, for example, she has a perpetually long list of what's wrong with her part-siblings or stepparent, you might ask some questions that cause her to recognize that she enjoyed it when she played Nintendo or pushed the baby in the stroller or helped make blueberry pancakes for breakfast. Or plant some small suggestions in her mind about how she might go about having more fun on the next visit. Help her get the idea, in other words, that there are things she can do—and should do—to promote a cheerier atmosphere.

HOW TO WORK WITH YOUR EX-SPOUSE TO SMOOTH YOUR ONLY CHILD'S WAY

It's not difficult to appreciate the wishes and the frustrations of the parent who has begun a new family with a new partner and truly wants his only child from the former marriage to be part of it.

During the limited time Angela's father has his daughter with him, he understandably wants things to run smoothly. Wouldn't it be great if Angela just naturally adored her new half-brother, if she instinctively understood that babies take a lot of work, maturely realized that her stepmother must focus all her attention right now on the newcomer? (And Angela, all the while, is wondering why she can't have Dad all to herself the way she used to and is feeling guilty that she's making her dad unhappy with her.)

If you are concerned that things often seem not to be sitting too well with your child during the times she spends with her other parent and family . . . if you are convinced in your own mind that that concern is genuinely rooted in your child's best interests . . . then it is necessary to take steps, difficult though they may be, to improve the situation.

TALK TO YOUR EX-SPOUSE ABOUT
WHAT'S GOING ON

Be in contact with your child's parent and let him know your concerns. Again, this requires keeping one's wits about one and not letting anger get in the way, a task that calls for strength and resolve. Angela's mother might wait for a calm moment (not just before or after Angela's weekend with her dad), organize her complaints into three or four specific recommendations for change, and initiate a talk with her former husband "to work out some ways to help Angela feel that she's a real part of your new family *and* that she has a special, separate relationship with you."

Their daughter might feel reassured—and take that new baby more easily in stride—if Dad makes a point of taking her, and her alone, out for a drive, a visit to the mall, a bike ride around the park. Many parents who are starting new families, I find, in their eagerness to get on with the new lives they have plotted for themselves, expect everyone to do everything as a unit. But fostering togetherness through activities doesn't always work. An only child, especially, needs the comforting reassurance of having her parent all to herself again occasionally.

If Ben's mother could go back to that time when her son was first trying to fit into his father's new household, she might have been able to help Steve appreciate what was going on with their son. He had been his father's only child, then suddenly two other children were vying for his dad's attention, children Ben was thrown together with through no wish or action of his own.

She might have said something like this: "I know you want to see Ben and he wants to see you, and I want to foster your relationship. But if he feels like a third wheel or left out of what's going on in your household, maybe in time he won't want to visit. And that's going to make him feel unhappy and guilty. So how can we make sure that won't happen? I know he's been a little upset after his last two times with you, because here is what happened afterward."

She might then have mentioned specific remarks Ben made or specific behaviors that indicated he was distressed—so that Steve recognized the feedback was clearly coming from their son and not from his ex-wife's perhaps vengeful imagination.

And then, ideally, both parents might have explored some ways to make Ben feel not so much like the black sheep among the three children. Even ensuring that the child had one place all his own in his father's home—if not a room, perhaps a closet or bureau or toy box—might have been a good idea. Knowing that no one else could use this special place when he wasn't there might have helped Ben feel more wanted.

SEEK SOME GUIDANCE

If one parent doesn't want to hear all this or doesn't perceive there is a problem or is unable, over time, to make appropriate changes—*and* if the child is clearly unhappy—the parent whose feet are on the ground and who's really monitoring what's going on with the child should suggest that both adults go for some outside help.

Again, help from an informed and caring but objective third party need not be an elaborate, expensive, or drawn-out process; one or two counseling sessions, in which both parents air their gripes, observations, or suggestions in the presence of someone else, can be enormously helpful.

While your child is adjusting to a blended family and a bunch of new people in his life, you'll help him a lot by trying to remain conscious of the small ways his life is changing and how he feels about that. Many parents who are establishing new lives with new partners, I find, take great pains to ease their youngster through the big changes, which they know can be upsetting if those involve a new house, new city, or new school. But those same parents can be quite unaware of how easily a child can feel dislodged by smaller changes in her home scene.

Until the new order of things settles down, both parents will do well to pay special attention to the small routines and rituals that help a child feel on familiar ground.

ONE FAMILY, TWO GENERATIONS OF CHILDREN

"She's very much an only child," says Marianne, the mother of seven-year-old Veronica. Veronica's father, Al, now in his mid-fifties, has three other children, all from his first marriage, which ended in divorce, and all now in their mid- to-late twenties.

"The older kids are always razzing her: 'Gee, *I* didn't get to take a trip to Cape Cod when *I* was seven like you did.' '*I* never got a swell dollhouse like that when *I* was seven.' Veronica takes all this teasing in stride," Marianne says, "because usually they're holding her upside down or tickling her or something when they're supposedly complaining about how much better she has it than they had it.

"And they take their responsibilities as big brothers and big sister very seriously in terms of educating her in the important stuff. They have to teach her all the gross kid things, like how to make burping noises and how to mash up green peas and stick them out of your nose so it looks like a booger."

Both of Veronica's parents love seeing the easy camaraderie that has developed among Veronica and her much older half-siblings. And relations among Al, his first three children, and his second wife are good.

For some older parents starting second families, the going proves more difficult. The father of a baby girl worries that his two older children, both in their late teens, are rightly resentful of the attention he showers on his new daughter.

"When my first kids were little, I wasn't around a whole lot," he says. "I was traveling much of the time, and then for a number of years before the divorce, their mother and I weren't happy together and I tended to get out of the house when I could. I love having the time now to spend with Sophie, but sometimes when the other two are with us they look kind of peeved. Actually, they like playing with the baby; they just don't like to watch me doing it."

There may be a determination on this father's part to "get it right" this time, to be the good father he feels he wasn't the first time around. And his older children may sense that and feel some bitterness.

If your only child has much older half-siblings or step-siblings in his life, how close they will all become will depend on that complex mix of personalities and history. But I would urge you to promote those relationships when and in whatever ways you can. Older part-brothers or part-sisters, even if they're only occasional visitors, may over time become rich additions to your only child's extended family.

As you and your child work out these new kinds of separated or blended families, there will be times when balancing your child's needs and your own needs takes a large measure of insight, effort, goodwill, and perhaps some occasional gritting of the teeth. Be reassured that only children are no less likely than any others to adapt successfully to the changes they are required to make.

· EPILOGUE ·

I was talking to a young neighbor of mine, a fifteen-year-old only child. "Do you think you'd like to be in a bigger family?" I asked Candace. "Have a brother or sister?"

She looked at me for a moment with genuine puzzlement. "What for?" she said.

We went on to have a long, animated chat about her life: her mother and father, her cats, her best friend in school, her worst enemy in school, her interest in baking, her efforts to work up a baby-sitting business in the neighborhood. Her parents, she said, "can be really irritating, but mostly they're great. We do a lot of good stuff together."

Sometimes, she felt, they were too strict with her. But she appreciated the fact that "they give me their reasons. And they always listen when I want to talk."

Something else she appreciated, she said, was that "I can always bring my friends home. My parents like meeting them. Actually, some of my friends envy me. They think my mother and father are terrific."

Later, I thought about how much I had enjoyed spending time with that young girl. She was bright, articulate, funny, and confident. She was comfortable in her own skin. Things in her life, by and large, had obviously gone well. I thought how nothing she said and nothing in her demeanor suggested she had suffered—in any way—from being an only child. And I thought how much she reminded me of so many of the only children I have known.

Children have been the focus of my professional life through many years of research, teaching, and working with families. How they develop, what helps them thrive, what steps they must negotiate on the way to becoming adults—these are issues that have captivated me for over twenty years.

In the course of reviewing the professional studies and talking to many only children and their parents in preparation for writing *You and Your Only Child,* I've been gratified—although not surprised—to discover that what the only child needs is simply what *every* child needs, no more and no less.

And you know what that is. Your child needs your love. She needs to feel secure in your care. She needs you to help her move ever further out from that core of love and security into the bigger world she will become part of. Now that you've finished reading this book, you know, I hope, that it is in your power to give your child all that.

I'm always interested in why parents read child-raising books. My own parents' generation didn't turn to books to figure out how to understand and bring up their children. There *weren't* many books available, for one thing. Those earlier generations of mothers and fathers relied on old rules (the way *their* mothers and fathers did things), perhaps on old wives' tales, perhaps on common sense, intuition, religious principles.

Many of those parents did wonderful jobs. At the same time, I think *more* parents today are doing even *better* jobs. Partly, we've decided that maybe some of the old "rules" don't work anymore (or maybe, in terms of what children need, they never were too sound in the first place).

Partly, we simply understand more these days about how children develop, emotionally and psychologically. We're less concerned that a youngster "be obedient" or eat everything on his plate (in fact, we know it's not a great idea to make him do so) and more concerned—appropriately—about his overall adjustment to life. We pay attention to whether he seems to feel good about himself and what kind of friend he is to other children and what his values are.

And partly, I think, we make better parents because we're willing to look beyond ourselves and our immediate families for ideas on how to help our children be the best they can be. In the last couple of decades, "parental education" has become credible. We're wise enough to say, "*Besides* relying on my own good common sense, my intuition, and my knowledge of my child, I'm going to find out the latest thinking on what parents can do to help children grow up well."

You've read this book out of that desire and willingness. And I hope you have finished it with new levels of confidence, awareness, and expertise. I hope that having explored along with me the many aspects of what it is to be or have an only child, you have banished any lurking worries that you won't be able to do right by your child or that your child is missing out.

I hope you have undergone a permanent and empowering shift in attitude, for that is the effect I most wish to have had: Stop viewing your youngster *as an only child* and consider him or her as your son or daughter . . . your family . . . your perfectly fine, healthy, normal family.

· NOTES ·

Chapter 1: You and Your Only Child

P. 3 Alfred A. Messer, "Parent and Child," *New York Times Magazine,* Mar. 19, 1967, p. 123.

Chapter 3: One Child . . . Not by Choice

Pp. 32–33 Denise Polit, "The Only Child in Single-Parent Families," in Toni Falbo, ed., *The Single-Child Family* (New York: Guilford Press, 1984), pp. 198–200.

Chapter 4: The Glorious Sibling

P. 48 "Busted: Birth Order Myths," *Child,* May 1995, p. 87.

P. 51 Jane Greer, with Edward Myers, *Adult Sibling Rivalry: Understanding the Legacy of Childhood* (New York: Crown, 1992).

P. 53 R. Carlson, *The Cain & Abel Syndrome: Getting Along with Your Adult Siblings* (Nashville, Tenn.: Thomas Nelson, 1994), p. 52.

P. 55 Victor G. Cicirelli, "Interpersonal Relationships Among Elderly Siblings," in Michael D. Kahn and Karen Gail Lewis, eds., *Siblings in Therapy* (New York: Norton, 1988), pp. 447–48.

Pp. 57–58 "Sibling Rivalry: It's as Inevitable as Death and Taxes," *New York Newsday,* Mar. 4, 1995, pp. B1–B3; "The Roots of Rivalry: What Sibling Friction and Fighting Are Really About," *Child,* June/July 1992, pp. 58–60; "Peace at Last: Sanity-Saving Tips for Ending the Sibling Wars," *Parent's Digest,* Summer 1993, pp. 95–96; "Resolving Sibling Rivalry: Surefire Strategies for classic conflicts," *Child,* Sept. 1993, pp. 122–23, 140, 148.

P. 58 Selma H. Fraiberg, *The Magic Years* (New York: Scribner's, 1959), pp. 280–81.

Chapter 5: Will He Be Spoiled for Life?

P. 67   A. A. Brill, quoted in Toni Falbo and Denise F. Polit, "Quantitative Review of the Only Child Literature: Research Evidence and Theory Development," *Psychological Bulletin* 100, no. 2 (1986), p. 176.

P. 67   V. D. Thompson, quoted in ibid., p. 177.

P. 68   Judith Blake, *Family Size and Achievement* (Berkeley: University of California Press, 1989), p. 7.

P. 69   Denise F. Polit and Toni Falbo, "Only Children and Personality Development: A Quantitative Review," *Journal of Marriage and the Family* 49 (May 1987), pp. 309–24.

P. 72   Denise F. Polit and Toni Falbo, "The Intellectual Achievement of Only Children," *Journal of Biosocial Science* 20 (1988), pp. 275–85.

P. 73   John G. Claudy, "The Only Child as a Young Adult," in Falbo, *The Single-Child Family,* pp. 211–52.

Pp. 73–74   Polit and Falbo, "The Intellectual Achievement of Only Children," p. 285.

Pp. 77–78   Blake, *Family Size and Achievement,* pp. 223–72.

P. 78   Toni Falbo, "Relationships Between Birth Category, Achievement, and Interpersonal Orientation," *Journal of Personality and Social Psychology* 41 (1981), pp. 121–30.

P. 80   Blake, *Family Size and Achievement,* p. 226.

P. 81   Ibid., pp. 230–34.

P. 85   Candice Feiring and Michael Lewis, "Only and First-born Children: Differences in Social Behavior and Development," in Falbo, *The Single-Child Family,* pp. 25–59.

Pp. 87–88   H. Theodore Groat, Jerry W. Wicks, and Arthur G. Neal, "Without Siblings: The Consequences in Adult Life of Having Been an Only Child," in ibid., pp. 253–86.

Chapter 7: The Family Triangles, Good and Bad

P. 119   Stanley Turecki, with Sarah Wernick, *The Emotional Problems of Normal Children* (New York: Bantam Books, 1994), pp. 174–76.

P. 127   Ron Taffel, with Roberta Israeloff, *Why Parents Disagree* (New York: William Morrow, 1994), pp. 32–37.

P. 135   E. Mark Cummings and Patrick Davies, *Children and Marital Conflict* (New York: Guilford Press, 1994), pp. 146–47.

Pp. 143–44   Judith S. Wallerstein and Sandra Blakeslee, *Second Chances: Men, Women and Children a Decade After Divorce* (New York: Ticknor & Fields, 1989), p. 33.

Chapter 9: Roots and Wings

P 174   "New Bonds: Para-Dads, Para-Moms," *New York Times,* Nov. 9, 1995, pp. C1, C10.

Chapter 10: A New Look to the American Home

Pp. 186–87   Wallerstein and Blakeslee, *Second Chances,* p. 175–88.

P. 187   Polit, "The Only Child in Single-Parent Families," in *The Single-Child Family,* pp. 193–94.

P. 192   Wallerstein and Blakeslee, *Second Chances,* p. 186.

Index

self-blame and, 189
siblings and, 186–188, 195, 197
taking sides and, 186–188, 191
triangulation and, 114, 116–117
see also custody arrangements; single-
parent/divorced family
do-gooders, 51
doors, locked, 119
down times, acknowledging of, 156–158
dreams, parental, 12

education, 72
preschool, 59–61, 166–167
religious, 151
underachievers and, 162–163
emotional balance, 3
emotional stability, 71
emotional wholeness, 143
employed mothers, emotional responses
of, 155
employed parents, down times of,
156–158
entitlement, sense of, 85–86
envy:
of friends' second child, 27–28
and only-child family, not by choice,
38
expectations, parental, 8, 13, 51–52, 74,
105–17, 158, 217–218
ex-spouse:
compromising with, 199–200
curiosity about, 195–196
remarriage issues and, 220–223
talking to, 198–199, 222–223
extracurricular activities, 175–176
superchild syndrome and, 151–152
extroversion, 71, 72

Falbo, Toni, 69–74, 80
families:
blending of, remarriage and, 213–215
emotional wholeness of, 143
extended, divorce and, 193–194
labels and, 48–51, 53
siblings as meaning of, 19–20, 38
single-parent/divorced, *see* divorce;

single-parent/divorced family
troubled, 20–21
two subgroups in, 11–12, 98
family roles, sibling identification and,
48–51, 53
family size, 1–4
guilt about, 25, 26–27, 102–103
see also only-child family, not by
choice
family triangle, *see* triangulation
fantasies:
about having a child of the other sex,
22–23
about having siblings, 4
parental, 12, 22–23, 52
father-daughter relationship, troubled
marriages and, 141
fathers, 4
as absent parents, 185, 190, 191
child care duties of, 126–127
feeling of being pushed aside in,
127–128
husbands vs., 7
in Oedipal period, 115–116
parenting styles of, 124–132
toddlerhood and, 115
father-son relationship, troubled
marriage and, 141
favorites, favoritism, 46, 52–53
fears:
divorce and, 191
in Oedipal period, 115–116
of parents, 13–14, 24–26
fighting:
conflict management and, 134–135
of parents, 133–135
of siblings, 43, 45–46, 58
finances, 38
first child, 48–49, 70
chronic illness or disability in, 38
grown-up behavior expected of,
217–218
only child compared with, 84
flexibility, 71
Fraiberg, Selma, 58
frankness about remarriage issues,
218–219
freedom, need for, 165